T0064234

DISCOVERING THE MISSING GOAL: SPIRITUAL DEVELOPMENT

Debra Dianna Thomas, Ph.D.

WESTBOW
PRESS®
A DIVISION OF THOMAS NELSON
& ZONDERVAN

WestBow Press books may be ordered through booksellers or by contacting:

WestBow Press
A Division of Thomas Nelson & Zondervan
1663 Liberty Drive
Bloomington, IN 47403
www.westbowpress.com
844-714-3454

ISBN: 978-1-6642-3461-1 (sc)
ISBN: 978-1-6642-3460-4 (hc)
ISBN: 978-1-6642-3462-8 (e)

Library of Congress Control Number: 2021909815

Print information available on the last page.

WestBow Press rev. date: 06/01/2021

DEDICATION

This book is dedicated to all those who have impacted my life. It is because of you that I have developed into the person I am today. Thank you all for your continued support regardless of what decisions—good or bad—I made.

To my parents, the late William Fisher Thomas Sr. and the late Thelma Henderson Thomas. Thank you both for instilling a thirst for knowledge and the willingness and know-how to seek that knowledge. Thank you, Mother, for being a strong and gentle soul who taught me to believe in God, in hard work, that with an education, my possibilities are endless, and that so much can be done with so little.

To my family, thank you all for always traveling with me on my many journeys. Although many of you questioned why I was taking my chosen route, you never discouraged me. I will forever be eternally grateful for your unconditional love and support.

To my friends, thank you for continuously entertaining my many seemingly unorthodox ideas. You never offered a disparaging word but were constantly extending an inspiring word, an adoring smile, a helping hand, and a guiding prayer. You all have cemented a special place in my heart.

To Dr. Willie Powell, thank you for your willingness to share the Word of God freely without forcefully expecting me to be where you were in the Word. Our time and talks have truly motivated me to want to know more about the truth through God's Word.

CONTENTS

PREFACE

Within this book, my humble beginnings are highlighted to demonstrate that all things are possible for those who believe in Christ Jesus. I have chosen segments of my life to demonstrate how although accomplishments were made, my life was still empty. Not until I was able to develop a true authentic relationship with God did my life change.

I pray that my story serves as an inspiration for you to seek wholeness!

INTRODUCTION

Becoming a "whole person" is a complex process. This complex process embraces many different factors. We must address our development in each of these areas: emotional, physical, spiritual, social, psychological, and professional. Although we tend to think that these areas work independently of each other, we must realize each of these factors impacts the another. Our "whole person" development intricately connects the different areas of our life and helps us to develop a balanced and prosperous life.

Our emotional development shapes who we are. This development is vital to our ability to recognize, express, and manage feelings at different stages of life and to have empathy for the feelings of others. The development of these emotions, which include both positive and negative emotions, is essentially affected by relationships with others, our ability to accept change, and our reactions to stressful situations.

Our physical development relates to our physical health. It includes eating the right foods, exercising to maintain a healthy body, getting enough sleep, and managing stress. We all know the importance of our physical health. It prevents disease, helps maintain a healthy body weight, and makes us feel good. Moreover, our physical health is good for more than our body. When we are taking care of our overall well-being, we are increasing our mental clarity, and we will have more energy to take care of our other responsibilities. Being healthy keeps us happy and confident, which results in contentment in other areas of our life (i.e., work, social relationships, and family).

Spirituality is an essential component of our development into a "whole person." It is a way of defining our purpose and connecting with ourselves and the world around us. Spirituality promotes compassion, positive relationships, a sense of purpose, honesty, optimism, and inner peace. These characteristics are often used in defining our success and happiness. We experience and express our spirituality for different reasons and in different ways. For example, spirituality is expressed religiously through the different forms (e.g., Buddhism, Islam, Christianity, and Judaism). Spirituality is also expressed through nonreligious ways, such as humanism, social action, and environmentalism.

Our social development corresponds to our ability to interact with others. Healthy social development allows us to form positive relationships with others. As we grow older (mature), we learn to better manage our own feelings and needs. We also learn to respond appropriately to the feelings and needs of others. Our social development is affected by our personality, the opportunities we have for social interaction, and learned behaviors.

Our psychological development relates to knowing our true inner self. As our childhood fades and we move toward adulthood, we go through many significant and dramatic changes in our development. Our psychological development promotes self-esteem and self-acceptance. Our relationship with ourselves is often equated to the most crucial predictor of success. After all, belief in ourselves builds optimism, determination, and motivation. It is these characteristics that ultimately leads to our success.

Our professional development is closely linked to our personal development. Regardless of where we develop ourselves (work or personal), that growth can be applied to every area of our life. If we are working a job that fulfills us, then we will feel a sense of accomplishment in other areas of our life as well. Our professional development is about more than just increasing or refining our skill sets. Our lives are enhanced by our ability to innovate and increase our overall potency within our chosen field by our willingness to grow and explore outside of our comfort zones. Therefore, our professional development is inclusive of our personal development.

To find balance, wholeness, and fulfillment in our lives, we need make some changes within ourselves. We must understand that all these aspects are equally important. Furthermore, if we want to feel "whole" and lead healthy, satisfying lives, we must devote time and energy to understanding, developing, healing, and integrating all six of these aspects into our lives.

FOLLOW YOUR DREAMS

Always follow your dreams,
Don't let them fade away.
If you lose sight of your goal,
It will haunt you some day.

Always follow your dreams,
As you shoot for the stars.
Nothing will be out of reach,
If you're willing to go far.

Jon M. Nelson

DREAMS

We all have had dreams about what we want to do when we grow up. We start early with saying any of the following:

- o "I am going to be a doctor!"
- o "I am going to be a lawyer!"
- o "I am going to be a scientist!"
- o "I am going to be a teacher!"
- o "I am going to be a singer!"
- o "I am going to be a rapper!"
- o "I am going to be a movie star!"
- o "I am going to be a professional athlete!"
- o "I am going to be a police officer!"

This list can go on and on. However, when we make these goals, do we consider the path and resources needed to reach them? Do we give thought to the notion of going to school forever to become a doctor, lawyer, or scientist? Do we consider the hard work and dedication it will take for us to become professional singers, rappers, and movie stars? Do we ever consider that there is a limited number of positions within the professional sports world?

Have you ever thought about why you chose those goals? What is it that makes you think that is what you want to do for the rest of your life? Well, I have a story to tell, and it starts with "When I grow up …"

BEULAH LAND

O Beulah Land, sweet Beulah Land,
As on thy highest mount I stand,
I look away across the sea,
Where mansions are prepared for me,
And view the shining glory shore,
My heav'n, my home forevermore!

Edgar P. Stites

Map of Bolivar County Mississippi
Designed by D. Thomas

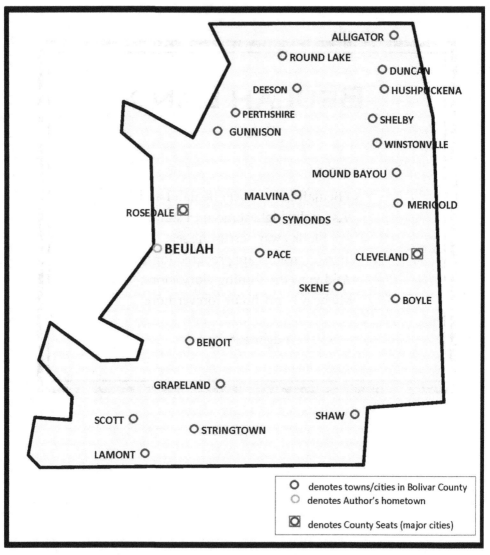

Map of Bolivar County, Mississippi.

Main Street, Beulah, Mississippi.

East side of levee in Beulah, Mississippi.

**RIDING ON THE TOP OF LEVEE WEST SIDE, BEULAH, MISSISSIPPI
PERSONAL PHOTO TAKEN WITH IPHONE**

Riding on the top of levee, west side, Beulah, Mississippi.

CHAPTER 1

WHEN I GROW UP

I grew up in the rural Mississippi Delta town of Beulah. Beulah is served by Mississippi Highway 1. Beulah is famous for Lake Beulah. A levee protects the town from an overflow of Lake Beulah. Lake Beulah, formerly connected to the Mississippi River, is west of the town. The Illinois Central Railroad had a station in Beulah, but the line is now abandoned. Beulah is named after the Christian hymn "Sweet Beulah Land." It has been rumored that Beulah was often visited by Mark Twain while he was writing *Life on the Mississippi*.

Life in Beulah was simple. There were few stores, no restaurants, and lots of churches. Beulah is located in Bolivar County, one of the poorest counties in the state. The demographics of the town include a majority of African Americans, eight White families, and even fewer Asians—a husband and wife of Chinese descent and their three sons. The majority of the people in Beulah were living below the poverty line. Every family in the town was poor, but you could not prove it by the way we lived. We went to Sunday school every Sunday and worship services every fourth Sunday. We never went hungry. We always had clothes to wear. No Jordans or True Religions, although we did wear Chuck Taylors. However, they were called by their real name: Converse All Stars!

I was born the fifth of sixth children. My father and mother worked on his family's farm. Later on, my mother worked within the Head Start Program. My mother always raised a garden. We had to get up early on Saturday mornings to gather the okra, tomatoes, beans, peas, corn, and any other vegetables that were in the garden. We got up early because we had to get our chores finished before we could watch anything on television.

I grew up during the time when the old adage "It takes a village to raise a child!" was the strictly enforced. The elders of the community had as much authority as your parents to guide you on the "right path." We were always taught that the only way we were going to make it "in this life" was with an education. We were not only pushed by our parents to excel in school; the entire community encouraged us as well. In many ways, the community celebrated our accomplishments as much as (if not more than) our families. School was not just an option; it was the *only* option.

There was no such thing as preschool, Head Start, or day care when I was growing up. The oldest sibling was the caregiver. There were no video games or computers to serve as entertainment. We were forced to use our imaginations. We played tag; school; red light/green light; Mother, may I?; Simon says; jacks; jump rope; ragball; and hopscotch. My favorite activity was to play school. I loved being the teacher and would not play if I could not be the teacher. Little did I know then that I would devote my adult life to teaching.

My whole family was big on watching sports. We watched basketball, football, baseball, bowling, and track and field. We watched the Olympics as a family. We all enjoyed watching wrestling (WWF) back in the day. We did not need video games or smartphones.

CHAPTER 2
STARTING SCHOOL

When I started school, the schools were segregated. I attended Beulah School, which only went to the sixth grade. Once we completed sixth grade, we were bussed to West Bolivar High School, the segregated high school, in Rosedale. Rosedale was five miles away. I attended Beulah School for first through third grade. We got to walk home for lunch every day. After my third-grade year, I was bussed to West Bolivar Elementary in Rosedale. I did not want to go to a new school; however, when I found out that the teachers from Beulah School would be moving to Rosedale as well, I felt a little better.

BOLIVAR COUNTY, MISSISSIPPI
COMPLIMENT OF RITA T. MARSHALL FROM LATE MOTHER'S COLLECTION

Beulah School.

My time at Beulah School allowed me to develop a love for my teachers. These teachers were so patient. Our class sizes were so small that sometimes, one teacher would have three grades in one classroom. If you were "advanced," you could be doing third-grade work, although you were in first or second grade. That really built up my self-esteem! I fell in love with school even more during those times. I think it was because I was the teacher's pet in many instances. I had four siblings whom the teacher had taught prior to me being placed in their classes. My family was known as a "prominent family" in the community. Therefore, I was able to become a teacher's pet early and often. Furthermore, my parents did not play when it came to school. You were going to do your best (getting A's and making the honor roll) regardless of how hard you felt the work was.

My teachers lived in our community. I was naïve enough to think that they were saints. You never saw them doing anything inappropriate, such as drinking, smoking, and going out on dates. They lived in the homes of the elderly or widowed women. The principal and his family lived across the street from me. His wife was my favorite. She would always let me grade papers for her.

While in third grade, I fell in love with my teachers. They always made me feel very special. I was a member of the dance troupe. However, I was not necessarily a good dancer. Ms. D and Ms. B worked with me until my skills improved until I was not so bad after all. At our school in Beulah, every year we would host plays— one for Christmas and one for the end of the year. When I saw the movie *Dirty Dancing*, I was reminded of our plays from the end of the school year.

I think it was at this time that I was running around saying, "I want to be a teacher when I grow up." My first goal was set. I had no idea what it would take to reach that goal. But what I did know was I wanted to be a teacher! Never knew how much money a teacher made, but I wanted to be a teacher! I wanted to be a teacher and live in the same town that I worked. Later on, it will be revealed just how comical this thought proved to be.

CHAPTER 3

ADJUSTING TO INTEGRATION

School bus.

In the fall of 1966, I was bussed to Rosedale to start my fourth-grade year. Rosedale was only five miles away, but it took the bus drivers so long to make that drive. We had to go over the levee to pick up children in the mornings and drop them off in the evenings. I would get home too late to watch *Dark Shadows* and Barnabas Collins. After watching the show, I would be scared to death.

The school appeared to be so big. There were trailer homes (Willis's Wagons) for some classrooms. We had to eat in the school cafeteria.

They served stuff like beets, carrots, broccoli, and asparagus. No one eats that stuff! The teachers made you eat all of your lunch and even drink your milk. After I left elementary school, I did not drink milk ever again. To this day, I still cannot tolerate milk. I have declared myself to be "lactose intolerant." No such thing was heard of back in my day. In the infamous words of Ike Turner, "I had to drink the milk, Anna Mae!"

West Bolivar Elementary School.

During my fifth-grade year, I had a teacher that you would love to hate, Ms. Right. She would make comments like "I do not blame you; I blame your mammy!" She never had a husband, and it was easy to understand why. She was just mean! If she felt the students did not want to learn, she put them in a corner and taught the rest of us. I learned a lot from her, especially how to bite my tongue and not let her have it when she started saying things that I felt were disrespectful. More importantly, I learned to deal with people I did not like just by being her class.

My oldest sister was attending the high school across the street. She would come across the street and perform some clerical tasks (typing, filing, etc.) for Ms. Right. One day, my sister made a lot of errors or did not complete the tasks to Ms. Right's satisfaction. Ms. Right talked negatively about my sister right in front of me. I wanted to say something inappropriate to Ms. Right. I would have gotten in much trouble if I had said to her what I was thinking. However, I could not wait to get home to tell my sister what Ms. Right had said. My sister encouraged me to not react to Ms. Right.

Ms. Right convinced my mother to allow me to stay after school once a week and go to Bible class at her church. Through my interactions with Ms. Right at the church, I realized that she was not so bad. I still remember making angels with clothespins in one of the activities at the church.

I had always liked sports. It was during my fourth-grade year that I started to play basketball. We did not have a gym so we played outdoors on a concrete slab. There was nothing fancy about it. For sure, there was no such thing as a three-point shot unless you got fouled in the process of shooting a two-point shot and made the free throw. We were not allowed to play five-on-five. We had six girls on the court at the same time. We had two defensive players who could only play the defensive end of the court. We also had two offensive players who could only play the offensive end of the court. Neither the offensive nor the defensive players were allowed to cross half court. We had two rovers. They were allowed to play both ends of the courts. I always played as a rover.

Outside basketball court.

CHAPTER 4

MAKING IT TO JUNIOR HIGH SCHOOL

West Bolivar Junior High School.

This style of basketball continued throughout my years of junior high school. Until I entered high school, tenth grade, we played this way. I will never forget when I played in junior high. We had so much fun. At the end of my ninth-grade year, Coach JC came down from the high school and spoke with us. He told us that next year we were going to play boy-style basketball (five-on-five full-court basketball). He then asked us if we were ready for that. Of course, to me that was a challenge. It was not until 1973 that girls could play five-on-five full-court basketball. When I entered the tenth grade, this was the first time that the state of Mississippi allowed girls to play "boy-style" basketball.

My junior high school had been the high school for the Black students prior to integration. It was the high school when my oldest sister and brother attended high school. It was built just for the Black students before the integration of the school system. The graduation pictures of my sister and brother still hung in the hallway. Looking at those pictures always gave me a sense of pride. However, it was not nice always having the same teachers as they had. The standards were set high just because of my last name. Comparisons between the two of us were common with comments like "Your sister was a nice, quiet, young lady! Do you know your sister almost failed gym?" Now I had found something that set my sister and me apart. I loved gym. It was the class that kept my grade point average up.

It was in junior high that I had my first White teacher. It was very different. Not all the teachers in Rosedale cared about the students. I could not figure out why they were teachers. I questioned that a lot when I found out how much they were paid. But guess what. I still wanted to be a teacher! The teachers were held in such high esteem in the community. Even though their pockets (and bank accounts were empty), they were looked upon as essential people in the town. Every family grew vegetables and fruits in their backyards. The families would offer fruits and vegetables to the teachers as tokens of their appreciation for the work the teachers were doing.

At home, my brothers (I have three—all of them older than me) had a homemade basketball rim in the backyard. It was made with a piece of plywood nailed to a two-by-four with a bicycle rim with the spokes removed. They would be playing basketball. I would go out there and want to play, but they would not let me. I would go to the back porch crying, telling my mother that they would not let me play. My mother would make them let me play. My brothers would be so angry. They would try to hurt me to make me go into the house. I withstood what they were "dishing out." It was at this time that I developed my mental toughness. My love for the game grew that much more.

Depiction of our homemade basketball rim.

My mother had been working with the Head Start Program since its inception in Rosedale. She did not have a high school diploma. To maintain her job, she had to get her GED. When I was in ninth grade, my mother passed the GED test. I was so proud that my mother went back and gained her diploma. My mother's accomplishment showed us that she was expecting something from her children that she was unwilling to achieve for herself.

My mother was very creative and crafty. Those skills helped her to be very effective in working with children. My mother worked in the Head Start Program for over twenty years. Witnessing the enjoyment that my mother received from working with the children was another reason why choosing to be a teacher made so much sense to me.

It was in junior high school that I developed a love for reading. I would read everything—including my oldest sister's *True Story* and *True Confession* magazines. I sneaked them from under her mattress, where she hid them. I learned to read very quickly so I would not get caught. I was reading fast before I ever heard of Evelyn Woods Speed Reading. Reading provided an escape of the reality of how life was around me.

Once I entered junior high school, every summer I had a summer job. I chopped cotton. I would go the cotton fields and work from sunup to sundown. (It was more like from 7:30 in the morning until 4:00 in the evening.) My first day on the job, I got fired for being literal. I chopped the cotton plant down and left the weeds. I was only fired for a short time and got it going again. However, I had it a lot better than my older siblings. The least I was paid for a day's work was $7; they worked longer hours and only received $3 for a day's work. The most I ever made for a day's work was $35. It was backbreaking work. I promised that I could not wait until I graduated from high school. I was never going to the fields ever again. I was holding onto my dreams of (you guessed it!) becoming a teacher and a basketball coach.

CHAPTER 5

OFF TO HIGH SCHOOL

West Bolivar District Number 1 High School.

Guess what I want to be when I grow up! You got it. I now wanted to be a basketball coach and a teacher. My mind was set, and off to high school I went. The high school was historical. It was the former school for "Whites Only" before integration. Only a select few Black students got to attend this school prior to the integration movement. Those were the "smart" Black students. When this occurred, we experienced "White flight"! All the White families removed their students from the school. The farmers and plantation owners built their own private schools and called them academies. The school serving Bolivar County became known as Bayou Academy. Whether it was divine intervention or not, many of the White students returned to West Bolivar because they were not able to keep up academically.

High school was fun. I excelled in my academics. Geometry was the class that caused most of my problems. I excelled athletically—in basketball and field events on the track team. The mental toughness that was gained from battling with my brothers in the backyard was put to good use. I learned not to complain so much and never put my head down. Those hard fouls that I had taken in backyard taught me to just get things done. However, this mental toughness kept my goals the same—to become a teacher and a basketball coach.

My youngest brother, W, and I were in the same geometry class. He liked that kind of stuff. I could not have cared less about angles or proving a theorem. Our teacher, Mrs. T, saw that I was struggling. She was always encouraging me. My brother's grades were higher than mine. Mrs. T would let me come in during my lunch to get help. My brother would come home from school and complete his geometry homework. He would then lock his geometry in his desk drawer so that I could not copy his answers. He found that very funny.

I fell in love with social studies after having Doctor J as my teacher. He was an old White man who would play "Dixie" on an old, beat-up, metal garbage can in his classroom to start class every period every day. Doctor J was ahead of his time. Who knew Doctor J was providing anticipatory sets for his students? He had never heard of Madeline Hunter. Doctor J had a way of making history come alive. Instead of focusing on dates and names, he focused on traits and characteristics of the people, which made the dates relevant. I served as his assistant for three years. This experience sealed the deal. I wanted to teach high school social studies, be a basketball coach, and get some letters behind my name (pursue an advanced degree).

Doctor J was beneficial in the continued development of my mental toughness. He was instrumental in helping me understand the purpose of a teacher. He drilled me on the importance of connecting with students, regardless of who they would be. I really appreciated the lessons that Doctor J taught me. He always encouraged me to stay focused on the goals and stay true to myself. I had Doctor J's wife as my math teacher in the seventh grade. She was one of the first White teachers I ever had. His son was my ninth grade government teacher. His wife and son were nothing like Doctor J. His wife was nice, but his son was boring. Doctor J was just different. He was very experienced and used it to motivate his students. I wanted to be like that.

My introduction to setting goals for my future came in high school. We set goals for everything. If you were a college-bound student, you had to complete the academic track. Furthermore, if you were a college-bound student, you were enrolled in typing and shorthand. If you were an athlete, you had to take the ACT during the eleventh and twelfth grades.

Another thing that I learned in high school was to make the best of my time. Making the best of my time meant being clear on what I wanted to pursue. I knew what I wanted, which was to be a teacher and a basketball coach. Because I was so focused in where I was headed, I did not worry about what other people were saying. And believe me when I say there were a lot of people who wanted to give unwanted advice and criticism. This was especially true when it appeared that I could earn a scholarship to play basketball in college.

As I got closer to graduating, I had been a two-sport athlete. I was on the track team, but my first love was basketball. I was no good at the running track. My contribution to the track team came through the field events. I was the number one baseball thrower on our team. (During this time, girls did not throw the discus or the shotput.) As a field event, I would throw a traditional baseball as far down a football field as possible. The person who threw the farthest was the winner. On a couple of occasions, my track coach had me run the 880 (two laps around the track) to get points toward winning the overall track meet. I finished the race every time but in last place most of those times. I am not sure how much help that was to the team!

As my high school career was winding down, I had some decisions to make. I did have the opportunity to go to college on a basketball/academic scholarship. Many of the coaches that our team played against sent college scouts to my house. I had the opportunity to sign with a couple of junior colleges or to attend Stillman College in Tuscaloosa, Alabama. I relied on help from my oldest sister and brother to help me make my decision. My mother left the choice up to me. She just wanted me to go to school somewhere.

Each of my siblings chartered their course in life. My oldest sister, A, had enrolled in a junior college that was offering me an opportunity to play basketball. She chose to move to Chicago and not go to school. My oldest brother, E, had an opportunity to go work for the FBI straight out of high school, but because none of his friends were chosen, he decided to attend Coahoma Junior College. After attending school for a 1.5 year, he chose to leave school and move to Chicago also. My second oldest brother, J, entered the air force after graduating from high school. My youngest brother, W, graduated from high school the year before me and was a student at Mississippi Valley State University. My youngest sister was just entering ninth grade.

I shared all this information to highlight I was not the first in my family to get accepted into or go to college. I am proud to say we all had a chance to pursue our chosen careers. I do feel that our choices made our parents proud. I am not sure if the paths we took to get to our chosen careers had the same effect.

For my high school graduation gift, my oldest sister and brother sent me a Greyhound Bus ticket to Chicago. I came to Chicago and stayed for three weeks. I was excited and, at the same time, paranoid and petrified. I had no desire to venture out to see anything. Everything that I had seen or heard about Chicago highlighted someone getting robbed, raped, or killed. That city's lights were just a little too bright for me. On the weekends, we did venture out to some of tourist attractions—lakefront, museums, zoo, etc.

Two of my high school classmates had moved to Chicago. They came over to take me out to dinner before I was to leave and return to Mississippi. They were bragging about how good the food was at the restaurant that they had chosen. We pulled into the parking lot of a fast food restaurant. They both announced, "We're here!" We were at "White Castle." I thought that I had missed something. They were talking about how good the hamburgers were. I could only smell onions. I did not eat onions. We still laugh about this outing to this day. At the end of my three weeks (Memorial Day weekend), I returned to Beulah to prepare to start at Stillman during the summer.

I was excited to be relocating to Tuscaloosa. I would not have to worry about chopping cotton ever again. I had never heard of Stillman College before visiting the campus in the late spring of 1976. Mr. Sam Merriweather, the recruiter, and Dr. Bettye Smith, the coach, drove to Beulah and took me and several other recruits (from the Delta area) to Stillman for the weekend. I had only heard of Tuscaloosa because of the University of Alabama and Bear Bryant. Bear Bryant's name was on everything in the town—Bear Bryant's new and used car lots, trailer parks, mobile homes for sell, Bear Bryant's Park, etc. Stillman College is a private, historically Black liberal arts college sponsored by the Presbyterian church located in the same town. I signed on to play basketball at Stillman College.

Announcement of signing with Stillman College.

Guess what, y'all! I had grown up (some)! I had put a plan (checklist) in place to track my progress to reach my goals. Something was missing, but I was not at a stage in my life that I could put my finger on just what that something was.

My Goals Checklist

Goal	Yes	No
Attitude	✓	
Artistic	✓	
Career	✓	
Education	✓	
Family	✓	
Financial	✓	
Physical	✓	
Pleasure	✓	
Spiritual	??	??

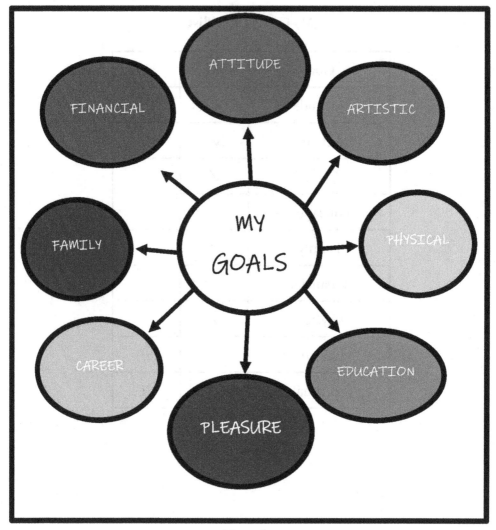

My goals.

CHAPTER 6

INTRO TO SPIRITUALITY

Depiction of Lake Beulah.

It was during this time that I had confessed my belief in Christ and was baptized in Lake Beulah. Acknowledging my belief in Christ Jesus was not an easy task. Since I could remember, it was mandatory that we attended Sunday school. We had Sunday school at Mama Lily's house or the church. I am not sure that Mama Lily could read, but somehow, she had memorized the Bible verses and was able to teach us what and how to apply the scriptures to our lives. Mama Lily was able to make learning the Bible fun and interesting. Then

Miss Mary became our Sunday school teacher. Although Miss Mary could read and write, her Sunday school lessons were rather boring.

The Holy Bible.

During the tenth grade, it was time for us to go to the "mourners' bench." Our church held a two-week revival in the summer of the year. We had to spend two weeks on the mourners' bench. No playing basketball, talking on the shared-line phone, or going outside for two weeks. That was brutal!

The "mourners' bench" sat in the middle of the front of the church during the revival meetings. Mourners and repenting sinners would come forward seeking salvation. The "mourners' bench" was the first step in the process of getting baptized and joining a church. We continually prayed for a sign from God that would allow proof that we had been touched the Holy Spirit. Some of us prayed for things like "to see a chicken cross the road" or "to see a cow on the levee at high noon." If you know anything about living in the south or near a levee, you know that these things happened daily. We lived at the foot of the levee. There was nothing spiritual about seeing these things. In reflection, this is a testament to the lack of viable Christian training we were receiving.

Depiction of the mourners' bench.

One year, my oldest sister and oldest brother got up from the mourners' bench and said that she had felt the Holy Spirit. My grandmother told them, "Y'all ain't got nothing! Go back and pray some more!" Because of this experience, my sister was never baptized as a believer in Christ. However, my brother did get baptized later during his adult life. At this time, we were attending a church located in a rural area.

Later, my mother moved our membership to a church closer to where we were living. On one occasion, my youngest sister was on the mourners' bench and she got off to watch the "WWF." She constantly spoke about being confused by what was supposed to be happening while she sat on the mourners' bench. Finally, my mother told her it was all about a belief—believing that Jesus Christ died for her sins. She only had to confess that she believed in her heart that Jesus had died for her sins and was raised from the dead.

As we were on our knees in front of this bench, other saints were praying and singing "Dr. Watt's" hymns. After declaring we had felt the Holy Spirit, we were now ready for a baptism. We were baptized in Lake Beulah. Yes, the very lake that I spoke about in the beginning of the book. None of the people (deacons, preachers, and others) knew how to swim. But we were out in the Lake Beulah. Let it be known that there was a history of large water moccasins being in the trees and near the banks of the lake. But for many years, this was where saints were baptized. I must dutifully note that during these baptisms, there were never any incidents or accidents.

Depiction of baptism in Lake Beulah.

My introduction to spirituality was robust. I had many questions and, in many instances, did not know where to get answers. My pastor was not one I could go to get answers, and the deacons would probably tell my parents. Therefore, the clarity and understanding I needed were left to me to figure out. I continued to go to church because my parents' standard did not allow for any negotiations. I would not even attempt such a discussion with either of my parents. Although my father did not go to church, anytime we asked him a question, we would get his patented answer "Go ask your mother!" I would not even think of that.

Depiction of country church.

My family's new church was a little better with the teachings. However, the preacher spoke so softly that we could not hear him. We only heard him when he said, "Huh! I can't hear you now!" That statement came after he felt he said something that should have moved us to shout or a joke that should have had us laughing. I wanted so badly to say, "I can't hear you either!" I knew better. My mother had a way of controlling us with that look that said, "You'd better not even think about doing it!" Even though I thought about it, I would never do it. The church purchased a microphone for the preacher to use. He was not any louder. I was at a stage in my spiritual development where I went to church because that was what was expected of me.

St. Peter MB Church, Beulah, Mississippi.

There was no doubt that I believed in God and Jesus Christ. However, was I supposed to be afraid of God, or was I to embrace God without the element of fear? How was I supposed to talk to Him? Did I have to wait until Sunday at church during prayer? Did I just recite the Lord's Prayer, or did I really talk to Him about what was on my mind? I needed more, but where was I supposed to get it? I had outgrown my box (being that little girl to do as I was instructed without asking questions).

Box You've Outgrown

What would you do?
And where could you win?
If these pesky walls
Weren't holding you in?

So, chase your big goals,
Beyond this safe zone
Step out of the box,
The one you've outgrown. (Gem @ the Goal Chaser)

31

CHAPTER 7

A STILLMAN TIGER

Dr. Smith and Mr. Merriweather promised my parents that they would take good care of me. They also promised my mom that I would most definitely be going to church every Sunday. I enrolled in twelve credit hours for the summer session. I liked the school and enjoyed my classes. It was rather easy. It was like a refresher from what I had just finished in high school. I enjoyed my teachers. I felt strongly that I had made the right choice by coming to Stillman. There were several employees of the college who were from the delta. They also adopted me as family—inviting me to family dinners, taking me to community events, etc. However, I still missed home. Life was different in Alabama from Mississippi. There were more unwritten rules for living in Alabama than living in rural Mississippi. The stores closed before dark, the radio station went off at six o'clock in the evening, and you needed a car to go anywhere.

I would spend time in Druid City Park, playing basketball with a couple of teammates from the area. A crowd would gather to watch us play. People would walk up and tell me how they could get me into Alabama State in Montgomery. I told them I would be playing for Stillman. I saw a lot of interest started to stir because women's basketball was relatively new at Stillman. That was fun. It was almost like we were marketing women's basketball at Stillman College.

It was at Stillman College that I got my introduction to Greek fraternities and sororities. At first, I did not understand why someone would subject themselves to the agony of pledging. For many students, it was a matter of keeping a family tradition moving forward. For others, it was a symbol of acceptance. I did not feel that was for me.

Although I enjoyed my eight weeks in summer school, it was time to head back home. Dr. Smith took me to the bus station. I boarded a Continental Trailways Bus to Leland, Mississippi, then transferred to the Delta Line (Greyhound) that would take me to Cleveland, Mississippi (home). I went home full of pride because I was a sophomore in college.

I arrived home from summer school on Friday afternoon. Excitingly, I shared my experience with my old friends on Saturday. I went to church on Sunday. When we got home from church, I heard some bad news: on Monday, I had to go to the field to chop cotton. I was so upset. I asked my mother why she was making me go to the field. She quietly replied, "You called home for a lot of things while you were away. Now you will make your own money!" I wanted to say, "But where is my college fund?" However, I knew that I would lose some teeth. So I had to prepare for my summer job on Monday.

I could not hang out with my friends because I would have to get up at the crack of dawn. What happened? I did not understand because I promised this type of work was a thing of the past for me. It did not matter what I thought or said. I had to do my part because it was not just about me.

I returned to Stillman in mid-August, ready to get busy. Because of my academic success, I was eligible to be inducted into the Gamma Iota Sigma Honor Society. I was so proud. The promises that Dr. Smith and Mr. Merriweather came up again. They promised my parents that I would be going to church every week. Little did I know that they would literally make sure that happened. We had a chapel on campus. Furthermore, every student was required to take four religion classes—the study of the Old Testament, the study of the New Testament, the parables of Jesus Christ, and the writings of Paul. A requirement for these classes was to attend weekly church services. If you attended the chapel, you had to sign in. If you boarded one of the community churches' buses you had to sign in.

The services on campus were short, but the singing was opera style. Now I grew up Southern Baptist. We would sing one verse many times to lengthen the song. Here, I could not understand the words that they were singing. This was why I did not like going to the chapel. I thought this would get me out of going to church. It did just the opposite. Stillman College allowed buses from the churches in the community to come on campus and transport students to the local churches. One of my teammates attended an AME church, so I would go to her church. It was much better. At least I could understand what they were saying. One of the ladies who worked in my dorm attended a CME church and I would visit her church as well.

Then basketball season started. We were terrible. Our team consisted of ten girls. Three from Mississippi (two from the delta and one from the Jackson area), four from Detroit, two from Tuscaloosa, and one from Georgia. The girls from Detroit did not go to class so they were ineligible. The girl from the Jackson area was ineligible. The girls from Tuscaloosa were nice people but horrible basketball players. They worked very hard. The girl from Georgia did not want to be there.

Our coach, Dr. Bettie Smith, was a sweetheart. She took good care of us. However, she was over her head with coaching a basketball team. Dr. Smith was older and coached as though we were still playing that "girl-style" basketball (four-on-four). For most of the girls, basketball was new. The girls from Detroit had "mad" skills but they could not focus on being student-athletes. Although we lost a lot of games that year, I was named MVP at the end of my first year. I would say that I was not the best player on the team, but I was disciplined enough to work hard and maintain my grades. However, I was still very proud of my accomplishment. I could not wait to get home to show off my "hardware."

I finished my first true year of college in grand style. I made the president's list. I earned the MVP trophy. I was ready to start my second year of summer school. I was very serious about earning my degree in three years. I was still working to become a teacher and a basketball coach.

Summer school was a breeze, but I wanted to go home. Dr. Smith died at the end of summer school. The team traveled to Dalton, Georgia, for her funeral. I really wanted to go home after that. I went home showing off my MVP trophy. Everybody in the community celebrated me. One of the store owners contacted Delta State University (DSU) out of Cleveland, Mississippi. The recruiter came to my house and convinced me that I should stay home and attend DSU. During this time, DSU was a powerhouse in women's basketball. I decided to transfer to be closer to home.

That was a big mistake.

By enrolling in DSU, I was reunited with the very people I needed to avoid. I lost focus of my goals. The promises that had been made by the recruiter proved to be a lot of "hot air." I started missing classes, my grades plummeted, and I gave up. Reality finally landed hard. My love affair with basketball was over. There went my goals and dreams!

Game over.

CHAPTER 8

DESPERATELY SEEKING
"WHOLENESS"

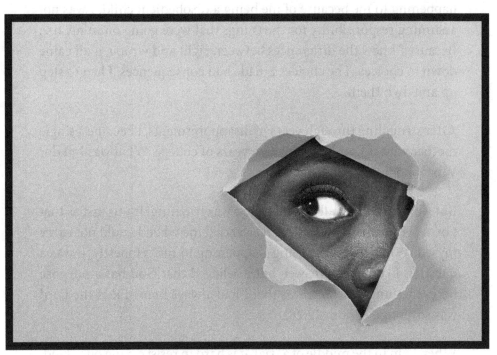

Desperately seeking wholeness.

Love has a way of playing mind games with us. When we think we have "found the one," reality rears its ugly head. It is at this point that what we saw as our escape route becomes our true nightmare. I moved to Maywood, Illinois. I struggled through many trials and tribulations, trying to figure out where I went wrong. I planned. I had goals. I kept asking the Lord where I went wrong. He would respond, "Where do you want Me to start?" I was continually reaching out to the Lord with questions. "Where are You, God? Why has this happened to me? What did I do to deserve this?"

I later learned that turning to God's Word (the Holy Bible) would help me get answers to the very questions that I had about why so much pain and suffering came toward me. Psalm 107:23–32 provided me some insight into God's role in various upheavals I faced. I learned that the Lord would often interrupt our lives by sending turbulence so that we will cry for His help. I accredited the things that were happening to me because of me being a disobedient child. I was not assuming responsibility for the things that were going on in my life. Because I knew the differences between right and wrong, it all came down to choices. The choices I made had consequences. I had to step up and own them.

After struggling through years of disappointments, I became a single mother with no career—only two years of college. What was I to do? What about those goals?

But when I thought all was lost, God was listening! It was just as that poem "Footprints" suggested. He carried me when I could not carry myself. Why were these things happening to me? Honestly, it was a question I could not answer, but I believed that God has a purpose for everything. My faith was that I had always known that the Lord was sovereign (Psalm 22:28).

When I am in the middle of a trial, it is hard to resist crying out, "God, why is this happening?" Sometimes I got an answer, and sometimes I did not. But I later understood that nothing happens by accident. I had His promise that He would cause "all things to work together for good to those who love God" (Roman 8:28 ESV).

As my son got older and started making bad decisions, I continued to ask the same question. "Lord, where did I go wrong?" I would always get the same answer. "Where do you want Me to start?" I am not bragging or boasting, but I have never hired a lawyer, put money on the books, or visited a jailhouse.

Seeing in advance how God would work all things for my benefit was very difficult, if not impossible. My limited human perspective often did not allow me to grasp His greater plan. The Father's good handiwork was in everything—even my pain, hardships, and losses. He turned my mourning into gladness and provided bountiful blessings and benefits from my darkest hours.

As a believer, I had to accept that things would not always make sense to me. Isaiah teaches that God's ways and thoughts are higher than my own (Isaiah 55:9). He sees the beautifully completed big picture. I could rely on the fact that God was in control no matter how wildly off-kilter my world seemed to be.

During this time, I was able to find a job working with students with special needs (autism) students at a school near where I was living. I had never heard of special education. Children like this did not go to public school in Bolivar County, Mississippi. These students were nonverbal and were learning independent living skills. I learned sign language to be able to communicate with the students. I worked at this school for about three years. I then transferred to a school for severe and profound behavior-disordered girls. I grew to love it there. In many ways, these girls reminded me of myself at that age. The only difference was my parents set strict boundaries and I had to adhere to them—no questions asked!

We would take the girls away from the local environment on camping trips where they had the opportunity to explore rock climbing, rappelling, teams' courses, and exploring caves. These activities helped the students to develop strategies to use when they found themselves frustrated. This Outward-Bound Program was powerful in helping the students develop trust in their classmates and staff members. I worked at this school for seven years. I also coached basketball and volleyball. Although all the students on my team were novices, I still enjoyed the experience. At this time, the itch to get back on track with striving toward my goals surfaced. I quit working at this school, went back to school, and earned a Bachelor of Arts degree in Applied Behavioral Science ("Management").

Upon completing my degree, I went to work for the Motorola Corporation. This was at a time when cell phones were becoming very popular. The pay was good, but the work was not fulfilling. I wanted to work with children. My thirst for being a teacher was returning.

One of my former coworkers from the alternative school invited me to go to church with her. I started attending church regularly. I had an awesome Sunday school teacher. However, I was living a chaotic lifestyle. I left church again. I was in the mindset that unless I changed the way in which I was living, going to church would not matter. Little did I know, I was really the problem!

I left the job at Motorola and went to graduate school to get a license to teach. I now wanted to be a special education teacher. I felt that "I wanted to be a voice for the voiceless!" The school I chose required that I get an elementary education certificate before I could get a special education certificate. I completed a master's program in special education. My goals were back in sight. I landed a teaching job in the local high school. After two years of teaching, I was hired as an assistant coach for the girls' basketball. I was well on my way, again!

I coached for almost ten years. That was a very fulfilling experience. After teaching in a self-contained behavior-disordered classroom for twelve years, I was pulled in administration. I became a dean of students (on interim level initially). I went back to school and earned a master's degree in Educational Leadership. I then became a full-time dean of students (loading up with advanced degrees).

As I became a full-time dean, tragedy hit. My father died. I was sitting in my office while meeting with a parent of a student who had been misbehaving at school. My cell phone rang. I usually never had my cell phone on at work. It was the day before Thanksgiving. My youngest brother was calling to tell me that my father had passed. My father had been sick; so it was not a shock, but it *was* a shock. I had just traveled to Mississippi to check on my father the month before. So we had not planned to travel for the Thanksgiving holidays. Regardless of your plans, God's plan is the one that gets carried out. We had Thanksgiving Day dinner at my oldest sister's house. We drove to Mississippi the next day because my father's funeral was going to be that Saturday. Everything was happening so fast. My father's oldest sister was home from Nebraska and would not be able to make it back the following weekend. In accommodating the elders of the family, we made the arrangements quickly.

As I reflected upon my father's life, I ended up laughing more than crying. As a little kid, I could remember sitting around my father (after he had been drinking) and listening to him tell his "war stories." Over and over, I heard how he got run over by army tanks in Okinawa. It was not until I got older that I realized what had taken place. My father had been a tank mechanic in World War II and he would be in a hole in the ground as the tanks rolled over for service and maintenance.

I returned to work at after my father's funeral with a new mindset. I needed to start to get my life in order. I needed to stop just going to the motions and really commit to doing what I knew was the right thing to do. I was continually being blessed by the Lord with promotions on my job. But I knew my priorities were not in order.

At the end of that school year, I received another promotion. I became the district's first director of special education. I initially thought it was a promotion, but it turned out to be a more of a curse. My motto had always been "I want to work *with* the children, not *for* the children." In this position, I was not able to do either. I had to research ways for the district to save money. I felt like I was cheating the students, parents, and taxpayers. These students were the most vulnerable population we served. Therefore, it cost more to educate them. Why were we trying to deny them their right to a free *appropriate* public education? After two years, I was demoted back to the classroom. I was not bothered by the move because, if you remember, I always wanted to be a teacher! However, I eventually worked my way back to the dean's office.

Four years later, I was still seeking my goal (advanced degree). I enrolled in a doctorate level program online. At the time, I only knew how to turn on the computer. I had to be out of my mind! At the start of my first class, my mother got sick. She then had a stroke. I prayed and prayed that I would be able to see her before she passed. I asked God to let her live long enough for me to get to Mississippi. For my fiftieth birthday, I went to see my mother. She did not even know who I was, but that was all right. God had answered my prayers. One week later, my mother passed. This took place over the span of five to six weeks. Never once did I question God as to why my mother had become ill. I just prayed that His will would be done. My mother was a very independent woman and to see her not being able to care for herself was hard. My prayer was for her not to suffer.

I continued in school during this time. Most of it was a blur. I wanted to quit, but I owed it to my mother to finish. I needed to finish for myself as well. I had started a lot of things and never finished, so I became determined to complete this program. In five years, I finished. I had earned my doctor of philosophy (Ph.D.) degree. I did not finish this degree because I was so "smart." I finished this degree because I had learned how to be patient and how to persevere. I am constantly telling people that I had three goals in life—to become a teacher, become a basketball coach, and earn an advanced degree—and I had reached them all. Nevertheless, I did not have a sense of wholeness. Was I overlooking something?

Have You Earned Your Tomorrow?

Is anybody happier because you passed his way?
Does anyone remember that you
spoke to him today?
This day is almost over, and its
toiling time is through,
Is there anyone to utter now a kindly word of you?

Did you waste the day, or lose it,
was it well or sorely spent?
Did you leave a trail of kindness
or scar of discontent?
As you close your eyes in slumber do
you think that God would say,
You have earned one more tomorrow
by the work you did today?

—Edgar Guest

CHAPTER 9

IS "WHOLENESS" NEAR?

Is wholeness near?

I became a grandmother two years before my mother passed. She was able to see her great-granddaughter once. My granddaughter became the apple of my eye. As she got older, she became active in things at her family's church. She was always inviting me to come to see her praise dance, her Easter program, her Black history program, her baptism, and more. I would attend, and I started to enjoy it. I started going more regularly. I have always been told that children are great "agents of change." My granddaughter provided me the push I needed to change my mindset. I started thinking about "earning my tomorrow!"

I fell in love with attending my granddaughter's family church. The people were very welcoming. It was a small congregation. My birthday present to myself was to find me a church home. I went to a couple of the local megachurches. I felt out of place. Whenever I went to church with my granddaughter, I felt right at home. As a birthday gift to myself, I decided to become a member, and I have not looked back. My action provided me such a relief. Now I know what was missing!

Attending the church services reminded of Mama Lily's Sunday school class. The teaching and preaching were made relevant. I was able to understand what was being taught. More importantly, I was encouraged to study the Bible for myself and not rely on others' interpretations. Regardless of how heavy the burden felt, I was welcomed with open arms at this church.

Through all of my trials and tribulations, God was always trying to get my attention. But I was not paying attention to His signs. I used to sleep with my television on all night. I had convinced myself that I could not sleep in a room that did not have a television playing when I went to bed. A close friend told me that sometimes God is trying to talk to me in the wee hours of the morning and cannot get my attention because of that noise from the television. I tried turning the television off. Since then, there has been a major difference in the restfulness of my sleep. I now look forward to hearing from the Lord during those hours. So no more television for me during the sleeping hours.

Although I had developed a plan with goals for myself, God's Word emphasized, "For I know the plans I have for you, declares the Lord, plans for welfare and not for evil, to give you a future and a hope" (Jeremiah 29:11 NIV). While God assured me that He had a special plan for my life and it was for good, it was not always easy figuring out where God was leading me. God may have been trying to reach me to encourage me, guide me, and lead me down a path of greatness. However, I was not always able to hear what He was saying to me. If I had wanted to know if God was directing me down a certain path, it became important that I paid attention to the signs. God was putting things in front of me so that certain things could become evident to me.

One of the ways that God was trying to get my attention was through my gifts and talents. The Bible says, "Having gifts that differ according to the grace given to us, let us use them: if prophecy, in proportion to our faith" (Romans 12:6 NIV). I had always been told that people who were in touch with their God-given gifts were one step closer to understanding their larger function in the body of Christ and fulfilling their purpose on Earth. As I looked inward and reflected on my life experiences, I remembered that my talent was working with children. I also remembered that I had that talent for a reason. I was to use my talent to glorify Him. Discovering my talents was not a process that required a lot of time and effort. But knowing my talent was necessary to achieving the life God intended for me. I felt that that desire to become a teacher was my God-given talent. God allowed me to nurture that desire and that goal. Being in pursuit of that goal made me a student as well. My talent has given me the richness of being a lifelong learner. As such, I serve as the superintendent of our Sunday school.

As I was desperately seeking "wholeness," my second grandchild was born. He is a very energetic little boy. He loves to run and jump. He likes playing football. He is such a sweetheart. When he was born, I was worried about the relationship we would forge. He has a way offering calm, and he is not aware of it.

God got my attention through my spiritual walk. It was imperative that I take my spiritual walk seriously. Second Corinthians 5:7 (NIV) says, "For we walk by faith, not by sight." Many of us seek God when we are in situations of need. I know I did! While this is okay, imagine a relationship where we did not focus our attention on what God could give us but how we could give back to glorify God. What a beautifully profound relationship that would be. I have learned to pay attention to the signs God has been, is, and will be revealing to me on my spiritual walk. I continually praise him for the past, present, and future.

Another big way that God tried to get my attention was through my passions, the very things I love. "For where your treasure is, there will your heart be also" (Matthew 6:21 NIV). I defined passion as the ambition that was materialized into action. I did not realize how natural passion was. I have found that sometimes I subtly overlook things that are staring right at me. I think about situations that have brought me excitement and joy, where I have been able to help others effortlessly. I discovered that the beauty of passion was that it was visible to me. When my passion was ignited, it helped me to influence the people around me and helped me to better serve the kingdom of God. I found my passion is constantly elevated when I seized the opportunity to serve others.

One of the greatest things God called me to do was give back for the sake of others. Often, God will get our attention through the very act of giving back. First Peter 4:10 (NIV) says, "Each of you should use whatever gift you have received to serve others, as faithful stewards of God's grace in its various forms." Matthew 22 also mentions Jesus gives us two commandments that summarize the laws and commands in scripture. One is to love your neighbor as yourself—a kind of love free of selfishness and expectation. The other is to love the Lord your God with all your heart, with all your soul, and with all your mind. When I used my blessings to help others, I was only advancing God's kingdom and practicing the love God intended for the world to practice. When I help others, many times they want to offer payment for my help. I constantly remind them that I did not get to where I am by myself. Someone helped me. So I ask that instead of paying me they help somebody else along the way.

Are you feeling called to do something that you were never called to before? Is there a goal you have had but you just have not completed it? Sometimes God tries to get our attention through the goals we have planned. God wants each of us to set goals for ourselves and actively move toward them. The Bible says, "The plans of the diligent lead surely to abundance, but everyone who is hasty comes only to poverty" (Proverbs 21:5 NIV). Just think, I had goals that I strived to reach for almost fifty years. The funny—or not so funny—thing is what helped me the most was not stated in a goal. While striving for the worldly goals, I realized I needed spiritual goals to carry me through. It was only then that my dreams started to become a reality. I never felt "whole" until I accepted that realization.

Scripture tells, "Seek the LORD and his strength, seek his face continually" (1 Chronicles 16:11 NIV). Prayer is important, not only because it strengthens our relationship with God but also because it is a place where God gets our attention. When I was not in a committed relationship with God and did not value the importance of prayer, it was easy for me to get distracted by everything going on in the world around me. When my prayers were not answered in the way I wanted them to be, my conversation easily went from "we" to "me". When I routinely prayed and listened to what God was saying, my focus shifted from the personal to the needs of others and I would better understand what God was telling me.

Lastly, one of the greatest ways God got my attention was through His voice. God wanted to lead me to all the good things He had in store for me. When I was having trouble hearing Him, it was imperative to remember that He loves me and wants to be involved in even the smallest details of my life. John 3:16 (NIV) is a great reminder of God's love for us. "For God so loved the world that He gave His only Son, so that everyone who believes in Him may not perish but may have eternal life." No matter how silent He seems, His love is phenomenal, and it never ends, even when I could not hear His voice.

Your life will be changed for the better when you can hear Him clearly and you know what He is calling you to do. Even when I did not know where God was leading me, I should have understood that He was constantly leading my path. Even when I had trouble hearing Him, I now know that God was still speaking to me.

CHAPTER 10

MISSING GOAL DISCOVERED

Thanking God for All That I Have.

Just as physical growth is vital to every human's life, so is spiritual growth in the presence of every Christian. A Christian cannot succeed and fulfill God's plan and purpose for his or her life if they do not embrace growth in the "grace and knowledge of Jesus" (2 Peter 3:18

NIV). A Christian who does not grow spiritually cannot be useful to God and cannot carry out feats. Through His divine power, God has "given us all things that pertain to life and godliness," but for us to experience these, it must be through His knowledge (2 Peter 1:3 NIV). If I want God's power to work through me and enjoy the fullness of God's objective for my life, I must partake of God's divine knowledge to enable me to grow spiritually.

God's most significant plan for His children is for them to imitate the image of Christ. Nevertheless, for this to happen, we must grow in grace and knowledge of Him (Ephesians 4:13 NIV). God commands to grow in the grace and knowledge of Jesus (1 Peter 3:18 NIV) just as the child of Samuel had to increase his understanding of God before he could fulfill God's purpose for his life (1 Samuel 2:26 NIV). We are individually responsible for our spiritual growth. God not only expects us to grow in grace and knowledge of Him, but we must continue in it, by applying His Word to every area of our lives so God can bless us in whatever we do (James 1:25 NIV). Measuring our spiritual growth by our material prosperity is a great disservice to ourselves. Prosperity not tied to the soul (3 John 1:2 NIV) is a recipe for death (Proverbs 14:14 and 16:25 NIV). As a bond servant, we must be willing to grow in His knowledge regardless of what it takes.

It takes divine or supernatural disclosure to know what God is about to do. Spiritual growth is not about the accumulation of knowledge of God's Word but the application of the culture in our lives. Having experience and not using it is a waste. To grow in the knowledge of God is dependent on the disposition of one's heart toward Him. How long a person has stayed or has worked in a local church does not determine their spiritual growth. Nor is it dependent on how active a person is in the ministry. One can be a churchgoer yet be spiritually stagnant.

Second Peter 1:3–8 (NIV) describes spiritual growth.

"His divine power has given us everything we need for a godly life through our knowledge of him who called us by his own glory and goodness. Through these he has given us his very great and precious promises, so that through them you may participate in the divine nature, having escaped the corruption in the world caused by evil desires. For this very reason, make every effort to add to your faith goodness; and to goodness, knowledge; and to knowledge, self-control; and to self-control, perseverance; and to perseverance, godliness; and to godliness, mutual affection; and to mutual affection, love. For if you possess these qualities in increasing measure, they will keep you from being ineffective and unproductive in your knowledge of our Lord Jesus Christ."

So spiritual growth includes an increase in a person's knowledge and understanding of God's Word, a decrease in a person's occurrences and harshness of sin, an increase in the repetition of Christlike characteristics, and an increase in a person's faith and trust in God. Perhaps the best summation of spiritual growth is becoming more like Jesus Christ. In 1 Corinthians 11:1 (NIV), Paul says, "Follow my example, as I follow the example of Christ." Jesus Christ provides the best role model for what it means to be spiritual.

For spiritual growth to occur, you first need to make sure you possess an authentic spiritual life through belief in Jesus Christ.

"And this is the testimony: God has given us eternal life, and this life is in his Son. He who has the Son has life; he who does not have the Son of God does not have life" (1 John 5:11–12 NIV).

Your faith in Jesus Christ is evident when the Holy Spirit lives inside you (John 14:16–17 NIV) and you are a new creation in Christ! Second

Corinthians 5:17 (NIV) points out, "Therefore, if anyone is in Christ, he is a new creation; the old had gone, the new has come!" The old nature, dominated by sin, is replaced with a new life that is under the influence of God's Spirit (Romans 6–7 NIV). You must acknowledge the Lord Jesus Christ as your Savior for spiritual growth to occur.

Spiritual growth is a journey that occurs as you read and apply God's Word to your life. Second Timothy 3:16–17 (NIV) emphasizes,

> "All Scripture is God-breathed and is useful for teaching, rebuking, correcting and training in righteousness, so that the man of God may be thoroughly equipped for every good work."

Several things must be in place for spiritual growth to occur. These include being taught, rebuked, corrected, and trained by God's Word. Then, we are thoroughly equipped for every good work. Being fit for every good work is the essence of spiritual growth.

Walking in the Spirit is another key to spiritual growth. Galatians 5:16–18, 24–26 (NIV) states,

> "So I say, live by the Spirit, and you will not gratify the desires of the sinful nature. For the sinful nature desires what is contrary to the Spirit, and the Spirit what is contrary to the sinful nature. They are in conflicts with each other, so that you do not do what you want. But if you are led by the Spirit, you are not under law … Those who belong to Christ Jesus have crucified the sinful nature with its passions and desires. Since we live by the Spirit, let us keep in step with the Spirit. Let us not become conceited, provoking, and envying each other."

When we walk in the Spirit, allow Him to fill you (Ephesians 5:18 NIV), control you, and guide you. Walking in the Spirit is brought about by consciously choosing, by faith, to rely on the Holy Spirit to guide you through word and deed (Romans 6:11–14 NIV). When a believer fails to rely on the Holy Spirit's guidance, the believer will not live up to the calling and standing that is provided by God's salvation. Ephesians 4:1 (NIV) states, "I urge you to live a life worthy of the calling you have received."

Galatians 5:19–21 (NIV) purports that spiritual growth is a lifelong process of demonstrating the acts of the flesh. The fruit in us is produced by the Holy Spirit. Yes, we are led by the Spirit because it is the Spirit who creates the fruit of our spiritual growth. When I started this journey, I kept trying to figure out what spiritual growth looked like. I found the answer in Galatians 5:22–23 NIV.

> "But the fruit of the Spirit is love, joy, peace, patience, kindness, goodness, faithfulness, gentleness and self-control. Against such things there is no law."

If you demonstrate qualities, such as being more loving, more joyful, more kind, and more self-controlled, it is safe to assume that spiritual growth is taking place within your life.

God works in different ways in everybody's life. Some people grow rapidly, while others grow slowly and steadily. The focus should be on comparing ourselves with God's Word rather than comparing ourselves to others. The scriptures serve as a mirror to expose us to what we are like spiritually and highlight areas in which we need to undergo spiritual growth. James 1:23–25 (NIV) tells us,

> "Anyone who listens to the word but does not do what it says is like a man who looks at his face in a mirror and, after looking at himself, goes away and immediately forgets what he looks like. But the man

who looks intently into the perfect law that gives freedom, and continues to do this, not forgetting what he has heard, but dosing it—he will be blessed in what he does."

I have connected the missing link of my chain of life development; I have discovered my spirituality. My spirituality development will always be a work in progress. I now better understand not only my purpose but also the road map that I am to follow. When I indeed declared myself a Christian, I entered a relationship with God, Jesus, and the Holy Spirit that will cause me to grow. With the power of the Holy Spirit, I am called to become more like Jesus. It is this spiritual growth that has become a birthmark of my faith!

"But grow in the grace and knowledge of our Lord and Savior Jesus Christ. To Him be the glory both now and forever. Amen." (1 Peter 3:18 NKJV)

I made it! I now have a real sense of where I am headed and how to get there.

Glory to God on High!
I am "whole!" I have a committed relationship with God through Jesus Christ!

Following Christ is not a casual for occasional practice but a continuous commitment and way of life that applies at all times and in all places.

Dallin H. Oaks

REFLECTIONS

As I strived toward spiritual growth, I had a lot of questions. Spiritual growth looks like what? Is it normal for me to have spiritual doubts or to question my faith? Is it all right for me to have questions about my faith? How do I know what God's will for my life is? I have spent many hours researching answers to these questions.

Question 1: What is the look of spiritual growth?

Edwards (2019) used the notion of how babies grow to describe the look of spiritual growth. He highlighted that babies progress through stages. Babies grow from being dependent upon their parents to many eventually becoming parents themselves. Our spiritual journeys are somewhat the opposite. We start off thinking that we are independent of God. However, as we grow, we acknowledge our complete reliance upon God and learn to count on Him rather than ourselves. Our acknowledgment is spiritual maturity. In developing our relationships with God, we recognize just how much we truly need Him. Nevertheless, it is not easy to comprehend the look of spiritual growth.

It is sad but true that many churches' and ministries' focus lies on getting people into the church, praying a prayer, and claiming the title "Christian." There is little or no aftercare offered. Although numerous new people come into the church and claim the Christian's title, many cannot recognize what a Christian is supposed to look like daily.

Committing to follow Jesus is not just a one-time decision. It is a lifetime decision. It includes a daily process of growth, and that growth is a biblical imperative. The expectation of scripture is not that we grow old together but that we grow up together.

Edwards (2019) offers ten descriptions of what spiritual growth looks like in a Christian's life.

1. You are learning more about God.

    When you love something, you devote yourself to learning everything about it. Imagine being married and not knowing the most specific things about your spouse. Not only will it cause havoc and chaos within the household, but it will also indicate a lack of love. We demonstrate an immature love for God when we do not study or grow in His Gospel.

2. You are digging into more profound theology.

    As children mature, their dietary needs also grow. Edwards (2019) borrowed the metaphor used in 1 Peter 2 to explain the maturation process. He highlighted that as young Christians, we start with the fundamental truths about God and His work. We are to grow our knowledge of these truths as we mature. All Christians must build on the foundation of these fundamental truths continually. We must be able to advance the concepts as we grow.

3. You are not waiting on others to feed you.

    Growing Christians should not wait on a pastor or leader to tell them what to think and what to read. Growing Christians should want more. They should most definitely seek a church with sound doctrine and Bible-centered preaching and teaching. To some extent, mature Christians can feed themselves.

4. You are learning and teaching.

    Edwards (2019) underscored the expectation of scripture as it relates to teaching. Scripture expects that, in time, all Christians should be teachers (2 Peter 3:18). All Christians are not likely to stand on stage and preach. However, a biblical expectation for all Christians is that we teach the Gospel. Teaching is not a gift given to all, but we all can help others grow on some level through sharing the Word.

5. You are growing in grace.

    Edwards (2019) emphasized that we should be growing in grace. Growing in grace means to share the heart of God. Our lives are to be characterized by grace. We should not seek justice or retribution against those who have wronged us. Forgiveness and grace should serve as our response and not anger or bitterness. Although there are times when people will not deserve mercy or grace, that is what grace exactly is.

6. You find yourself wanting to obey God.

    Edwards (2019) pointed out that a maturing Christian is naturally faithful and obedient to God's commandments. We do this not out of duty but out of love for Him. John 14:15 provides evidence to support this claim.

7. You are growing as a person.

    Edwards (2019) highlighted that the apostle Paul spoke about bearing fruit in his letter to the Colossians (Colossians 1:10). The apostle Paul also identified the fruit of the Spirit in his letter to the Galatians (Galatians 5:22–23): love, joy, peace, forbearance, kindness, goodness, faithfulness, gentleness, and self-control. Examining the fruit in our lives is one of the best ways to measure our growth. Because we are all different, we will see some fruit growing more effortlessly than others. For example, self-control may be more effortless for one person with ease and be the most challenging for another person. It is imperative that your fruit is visible to others and not just to you in your self- examinations. Strangers should be able to see these fruits growing in our lives. If other people cannot verify this fruit in our lives, then we might be misleading ourselves because our fruit is not growing as much as we think it is.

8. You are less worried about personal preferences and more concerned about unity.

    In his letter to the Ephesians (Ephesians 4:13–15), the apostle Paul noted the measures of fullness in Christ are evident through the harmony of the faith and knowledge of Jesus. Edwards (2019) accented that the challenges of personal preferences prevalent within American Christianity demonstrate a lack of maturity. Although it is not illegal to share a mixture of styles within churches, the extent to which expectations and efforts are evoked based on personal preferences to make changes can cause a significant lack of unity.

9. You are willing to speak the truth in love.

    In Ephesians 4:15–16 (NIV), Paul teaches us to speak the truth in love and grow in Christ, making the whole body grow in love. Edwards (2019) noted that Paul addressed our culture's obsession with avoiding conflict. Yet it is God's truth. Becoming confrontational when disagreeing with someone is not equated to speaking the truth in love. The more we grow spiritually, the better we will become in addressing challenging topics with other believers. We will be able to speak with loving humility and grace.

10. You are engaged in community.

    Edwards (2019) emphasized that we are encouraged to continue to meet regularly. He noted that the writer of the book of Hebrews encouraged us to meet regularly. With the contemporary church, it seems as though we live in a culture that moves further and further away from regular church involvement. The Bible teaches that growing and maturing Christians will continually and consistently meet and create a sense of community.

It is easy to take on the title "Christian." It is easy to remain dormant because growing takes work. We must be intentional about growing spiritually.

The Gospel is like a workout routine: the more we engage in it, the more it will change our lives. Participating only once a week means that it will take longer to see some desirable outcomes. Our love for God should compel our growth in knowledge and comprehension of Jesus to become more like Him.

Question 2: Is it acceptable for me to have questions about my faith?

Hertzenberg (2020) emphasizes that for many people "religion is simply meant to be accepted. That is why it is called faith." Hebrew 11:1 (NIV) defined faith as the "confidence in what we hope for and assurance about what we do not see." Therefore, for these peoples, questions and doubts about faith can only belong in the secular world, not religion. None of us have the right to question God. To question morality is to question God, and questioning God is immoral. Those who have questions about their religion are said to be lacking in their faith. If they were strong and confident in their faith and indeed followed God, there would be no questions. So encouraging them to focus more fully on God is the only way to deal with the questioning minds. They will no longer need to question their faith if they were to strengthen it. Many times, questioning one's faith does not always go as planned. A person who asks serious questions about their religion does not want to hear clichés and commonplace responses.

Although they have honest concerns and sincere questions, they do not want to feel that they are not valid. They want accurate and truthful answers, even if the answer is "I do not know, but I can find out." Essentially, they need to either be given the answers or given directions on locating the answers to their questions, especially if they will continue to strive for growth within their faith.

The people who are questioning their faith are not usually looking for excuses to leave religion behind. In many instances, it is often just the opposite. Many people who ask questions about their faith seek answers to justify their continuing to practice their religion. They are seeking validation to remain faithful, and you should treat them as such. They should acknowledge and trust that their faith does have the answers they seek—if someone would just help them find those answers rather than labeling them as being weak in faith.

Regardless of how many religious communities react to people who have questions about their faith, there is nothing illegal about having questions about your faith. In many orthodox circles, curiosity is a bad thing. Although curiosity may occasionally only get lip service, genuine interest in their faith needs attention in practice. Some claim to support curiosity concerning their faith. However, they only want people to ask questions about faith that spiritual leaders can answer. They do not want to deal with the higher-order thinking question, which is the hallmark of genuine curiosity. The follow-up question to this is: "Why?"

A significant characteristic of a person's personality is curiosity. Wondering why a person feels the way they do causes curiosity to lead to empathy. Curiosity can promote growth in the lives of others. In many instances, curiosity appears in the form of questions. A common question that many potential volunteers ask themselves before volunteering is "How can my volunteerism help the people in my community?"

In many instances, curiosity is the cause of people getting in trouble when it comes to faith. People are curious about topics. Among these topics are sex, vice, and sin. Sometimes, this curiosity leads them to go awry. They should simply seek guidance from those who are more knowledgeable of the Gospel.

While this can be true in some instances, this dismal picture of curiosity leaves out the good that can result from questioning your faith. A person who has questions about their faith will become very persistent because they genuinely want to get answers. To get the desired responses, they will begin to investigate their religion seriously. While that idea may cause some to become agitated, a person who truly studies their faith often starts with the resources they are most familiar with using. Therefore, they will begin by carefully examining the texts they grew up reading and talking to the spiritual authorities they were taught to respect. For example, most Christians would start investigating Christianity by conducting a closer reading of the Holy Bible. These Christians would seek a deeper meaning of each scripture. The knowledge gained will help to garner a better understanding of Christ's teachings. The curious Christian might then try to learn more about the time Jesus lived. These facts could help them gain a better context of some of the events in the Bible. It would also help provide a perspective from which to understand the developments within the Old Testament better. A simple question supported by genuine curiosity can lead a Christian to a deeper comprehension of the Bible's sixty-six books. This action is far from leading the Christian to the abandonment of their faith. Because of how curiosity feeds itself, the Christian could also likely form new questions that lead him or her to dig even deeper into their faith.

Questions can lead a person to become much more knowledgeable about their faith. Answering these questions can also direct the path of growth for a person in their faith. A person who has never questioned anything about their religion is like a tree growing in a gentle climate. Although the tree may stand tall, its roots are shallow. However, someone who questioned faith and found satisfactory answers, on the other hand, is a tree that has survived many storms.

Each answered question leads the Christian to believe in their faith that much more. After all, their faith provided the answer to each question, which often leads to other questions. Maintaining the tree metaphor, consider which of these two trees are more likely to survive when one of life's hurricanes rolls ashore: the shallow-rooted tree that was never truly challenged or the tree subjected to trial and grown deep roots.

Overcoming challenges makes some things steadfast. Regardless of whether it is a person's mind, body, or faith subjected to a trial, this is a valid statement. Things that can survive struggles will last, and things that can hold up under scrutiny are more likely to be believed and trusted. Intrinsically, there is nothing wrong with a person questioning their faith. Moreover, it is through questions that a person learns and grows. Furthermore, through finding answers, a person gains the confidence to say without fear or stipulations, "I believe!"

Question 3: Is it acceptable for me to have spiritual doubts?

Experiencing spiritual doubts can be very scary. When you have severe spiritual doubts, you will question nearly everything you ever knew. These doubts can cause you to feel lost in a world that is becoming more and more unfriendly. Nevertheless, when you suddenly start to doubt whether God exists, you begin to ask what the point of anything is. Why are you living if there is no life after death? Why do your actions and reactions matter? Why do morals and ethics matter? All spiritual doubts are uncomfortable regardless of what degree they exist.

Questioning your spirituality is uncomfortable because they force you to question things that you were always taught and not meant for questioning. Faith says to be just that—taken on faith. Abruptly questioning your beliefs can make you feel like you are overstepping your boundaries. You are mere mortals, mere humans. Therefore, who are you to question God? Furthermore, spiritual doubts make you feel like you are against God; spiritual doubts also make you feel like you turn your back on your family and friends. While your family and friends demonstrate comfort in their faith, you are experiencing difficulties relating to them because of their devout faith.

Although you may feel guilty about having spiritual doubts, there is nothing wrong with having indecision periods. Having spiritual doubts does not mean that you have left your faith behind. Moreover, having spiritual doubts provides a way to grow and fortify your faith. The lack of spiritual doubt makes you unlikely to question anything about your faith openly and honestly. Still, you would probably be satisfied with platitudes or simple surface answers. People do not usually push for a severe reply unless there is an actual question. "I wonder" or "I am curious" does not always have the necessary power to push you to investigate what you believe honestly. However, the question "What if I am wrong?" can give people an enormous push to prove themselves right. "What if there is no God?" then becomes how people demonstrate to themselves, and possibly others, that there is indeed a God. The person who doubted then becomes a more profound believer. Furthermore, the person has gathered confirmation that can potentially help others who are having similar questions.

The kind of self-reflection that having spiritual doubts establishes may expose the faith areas you had not known existed. To dismiss one doubt might require that you focus your attention on something else. Later investigations will need to now concentrate on this new detail. For example, you may have questions about what constitutes a sin. You will ask questions like "Is watching pornography a sin?" As you search through the Bible for verses that could help you answer your questions, you might find another scripture that grabs your interest or even confuses you more. Perhaps you stumble upon a reference to the Pharisees. You question who the Pharisees were in biblical times and why they were on such a warpath. After you have addressed your question about pornography, your curiosity now focuses on the Pharisees as you read more into Jerusalem's history during the Roman period and learn about the various traditions that competed for followers. Your curiosity helps you to acquire a greater understanding of the context in which Jesus was preaching. This context then allows you to find a deeper meaning or clarify verses and other confusing events to you in the past.

Spiritual doubts also help you indeed come to own your faith. If you never doubt or seek clarity, you will never honestly understand why you believe what you allege you believe. Without ever genuinely questioning why your beliefs matter, you will continue to believe what you thought you need to believe. In many instances, the doubts you face will not have to be momentous. Insignificant details relating to doctrines can lead to questions that cause you to conduct a more in-depth study. The answers you discover during this study help you come to terms with your faith.

As awkward as they are, spiritual doubts also allow you to endorse your faith to others. Questioning your faith prepares you with the ability to defend your faith. When others question your beliefs, you uphold your beliefs. Your answers and defenses will seem superficial and clichéd to the person who is challenging you. They will feel that you are following carelessly and never attempted to consider the full meaning or implications of what you believe.

Never really questioning your faith means you will never be able to defend it completely. When others question your beliefs, you uphold your beliefs. Your answers and defenses will seem superficial and clichéd to the person who is challenging you. They will feel that you are following aimlessly and never attempted to consider the full meaning or implications of what you believe. Being able to defend your belief may seem like a minor detail, but if you cannot even protect your faith from questions, how can you convince anyone else to follow it? If you do not transform people, one bad experience is enough to turn someone who was considering transformation off forever. Because you readily accepted everything and never experienced doubts or questioned your faith, the person trying to convince you of the need for change may assume that your faith is telling you that all believers should follow blindly. Most people stray away from a religion that purports this type of reputation.

Wrestling with spiritual doubts is awkward and unpleasant and can be very frightening. It can appear as being disloyal to everything you ever believed and everything you ever learned. Spiritual doubts are not a disaster, regardless of how awful they may seem. Spiritual doubts are opportunities to grow in your faith and to learn more about what you believe. They are chances to honestly examine your faith so that you can openly and sincerely declare, "I believe this, and here is why." Faith devoid of any doubts is blind, but faith that endured doubts is like a tree that survived a hurricane. It goes under in its roots and stands tall through even the worst storms.

Question 4: How do I know God's will for my life?

Whether you realize it or not, God has a purpose for your life. The reason that you are alive on this planet is your purpose. Not sure whether you have a goal or not? Stop for a moment and take a breath. Are you breathing? Then yes, you do have a purpose. A specific plan and will have been devised for your life by God.

There are many questions relating to knowing God's will for our lives. Some of these questions are "How can you know God's will for your life?" and "When do you find your purpose?" One point that is difficult to accept as an answer is finding it when you find it. Your

DEBRA DIANNA THOMAS, PH.D.

purpose does not find you. You must be intentional in your search for it.

Another difficult question is "Why is God's will so hard to find?" The answer is that nothing worthwhile is easy, and the process of discovering your purpose increases its value in your life. Proverbs 25:2 (NIV) states, "It is the glory of God to conceal a matter; to search out a matter is the glory of kings." Discovering what God has concealed, including our purpose, is one of the highest honors we have.

Many of us fail to discover God's will because we are so easily distracted. In the end, God's will matters because we want our lives to matter. In Jeremiah 29:11 (NIV), God promises, "'I know the plans I have for you,' declares the Lord." Nonetheless, the question remains "How do I begin to discover God's will for my life?"

You will never be able to redeem your future if you stay focused on your past and hold onto the old you (before you knew God). Redeeming your past is not just forgetting it. Redeeming your past is finding value in even your most incredible pain and heartache because one of the things you will encounter when you find your purpose is that your most significant purpose comes from your most tremendous pain. You need to redeem your past.

Your parents or maybe a teacher might have asked you, "Why can't you be more like your brother or sister?" But you are not. You are who you are. Are you an introvert? An extrovert? Are you people oriented? Task oriented? All those helps make you who you are, and you need to know your personality. Your design helps reveal your destiny. You can utilize online tests that can help you discover your personality. God has uniquely created you. Celebrate the person you God designed you to be.

The Spirit gives you spiritual gifts and divine opportunities to make a difference in your world when you trust in Jesus and allow the Holy Spirit to dwell within you. You need to know your spiritual gifts. These gifts link directly to your personalized purpose. Romans 12:5–6 (NIV) states,

> "So in Christ, we, though many, form one body, and each member belongs to all the others. We have different gifts, according to the grace given to each of us."

Discovering your God-given spiritual gifts helps you find your life's purpose. I found a web site (www.spiritualgiftstest.com) that provides a great place to start exploring your spiritual gifts.

There is more to discovering your purpose than just taking a bunch of tests. It is beginning to venture out and do some field-testing on what you think your purpose might be. You will discover when you start to probe into finding your purpose because living your purpose is not an accident. God has divinely orchestrated events and circumstances in your life to present you with opportunities to live out your purpose. We tend to spend time looking for things that are right in front of our faces. We need to open our eyes, closely examine, and begin to see the circumstances around us. Too often, many Christians stumble their way through life, never lifting their eyes to see beyond their own feet. Walk with your eyes wide-open, and begin discerning the opportunities lying right in front of you.

More importantly, you need to take advantage of the opportunities right in front of you. For example, you might convince yourself that your divine purpose is to become something totally outside of a rocket scientist, but some outside counsel would help point out the flaws in your theory if you never finished high school. You are not on a solo mission when you are working to discover your purpose. Wise and discerning people have been placed in your life by God to aid you in finding your purpose. The wisest person to ever live,

Solomon, spoke more about seeking wise counsel than anyone else. Proverbs 19:20 (NIV) says, "Listen to advice and accept discipline, and at the end, you will be counted among the wise." Proverbs 13:10 (NIV) says, "Wisdom is found in those who take advice." We all need to be surrounded by a few people who can offer wise counsel into our lives. We must find these people and rely on their counsel.

Through it all, ask God. Ask Him every day, along every step. God wants us to begin to live our redemptive purpose, and He wants us to discover it. God wants us to depend on Him throughout our spiritual growth process because He wants us to grow intensely in our relationship with Him. That is the whole point. The hard work that we do in discovering our purpose will be precious because it will rejuvenate our entire lives.

Your purpose is important because you are important, and your life is important too. You can begin your life-giving, soul-filling, eye-opening adventure of discovering your God-given purpose.

Putting on the Full Armor of God

During my quest for spiritual growth, I reflected upon the many battles I fought against the Enemy. I now know that once I started to study the Bible, I equipped myself with the "full armor of God."

As I struggled with understanding how to become a more spiritual person, I failed to realize that my number one battle was taking place in my head. The Bible (2 Corinthians 10:3–4 ESV) tells us,

> For though we walk in the flesh, we are not waging war according to the flesh. For the weapons of our warfare are not of the flesh but have divine power to destroy strongholds.

I had to realize the battles were taking place in my thoughts. My actions provided the Devil the opportunity to attack me daily. Until I took refuge in countering the Devil's attacks through studying the Bible, I was always under attack.

As I searched for my spirituality, several biblical verses led me to the awareness that I needed to become "whole." The Enemy will attack you when you are in a weak position, both physically and emotionally. The Enemy attacked Jesus after He had fasted for forty days. Scripture tells us,

> "After fasting forty days and forty nights, he [Jesus] was hungry. The tempter came to him and said, if you

are the Son of God, tell these stones to become bread"
(Matthew 4:2–3 NIV).

The Devil tried to attack Jesus when He was physically at one of
his lowest points. At one time in my life, I nurtured my weaknesses
and kept them. I entangled myself in the web that had been spun by
the Devil. The Devil had his grasp on me, and I willingly allowed
him to keep me by having my pity parties. Thankfully, I went to the
scriptures that speak to God's excellent assurance.

> "Finally, be strong in the Lord and His mighty power.
> Put on the full armor of God, so that you can take
> your stand against the Devil's schemes" (Ephesians
> 6:10–11 NIV).

During this time, I was always tired and sluggish. I attributed my
lack of energy and vitality to the extended attack by the Devil. There
were other possible reasons for my fatigue, including the inability
to sleep, lots of headaches, and digestion problems. However, when
I was in this state, I could not do the things God had called me to
do. I came to understand that there is liberation in waiting, resting,
and relying upon God and not man. God's Word reminds us of
God's protection during a spiritual attack. "But the Lord is faithful,
and he will strengthen you and protect you from the evil one" (2
Thessalonians 3:3 NIV).

When I decided to make some changes in my life, I always felt
attacked by the Devil. There is nothing that the Devil dislikes more
than building your relationship with God and growing in your faith.
Right after the Devil attacked Jesus, He began His public ministry.
The Bible tells us, "From that time Jesus began to proclaim. 'Repent,
for the kingdom of heaven has come near'" (Matthew 4:17 NIV).

The Devil attacked Jesus because he knew that Jesus was about to
start His ministry. However, Jesus was not discouraged. Several

friends warned me that once I started on my new spiritual journey, the Devil would be attempting to sabotage and distract me from growing closer to God. The Devil did not want to see me expanding the mission of Christ. Determined, I would not let the Devil defeat me. I remembered that the spiritual weapons that God provides us have astonishing power.

When I first moved to Maywood, I became very frustrated. Nothing seemed to be going right. I thought it would be prosperous and provide joy and happiness, but it offered nothing but agony, pain, and frustration. I later learned that I was prime picking for the Devil. The Devil attacked when I was going through my period of extreme frustration. He used a variety of circumstances to dominate my mind and helped to generate much of my frustration. I was under siege by the Devil. I found myself always feeling on edge, anxious, and agitated. During these times, a simple conversation grew into a massive confrontation. I was still on the defense about everything. Most of my thoughts were always negative. This attack had moved from being thoughts in my head to me acting on them. I had to find something different to focus on because I had gotten so bad that no one wanted to be around me. I started to focus on God. I placed myself on guard.

When I was living a chaotic life, I started going to church for a short while. I did not change my lifestyle, but I was going to church. The Devil attempted to entice me to believe that I did not need to change anything. I was hurting physically, emotionally, spiritually, socially, psychologically, and professionally. The Devil tried to convince me that everybody else was the problem, not me. The Devil tried to persuade me that God was not concerned about me. The Devil was continually telling me, "Hey, I got this! You are all right!" But I was not all right. He wanted me to believe that he had all the answers. As I reached out to God, the Devil made it seem like no one listened to me. Yet God was telling me to follow His Word.

While discovering my spirituality, I made some hard decisions to change some habits and lose some friends. Therefore, I was spending a great deal of time alone. Once again, I became a prime candidate for the Devil's attacks. The Devil knows that we are most vulnerable when we are by ourselves. The Devil knew Jesus was alone, and he tempted Him. I felt that the Devil could sense when I am feeling lonely. During his attacks, the Devil wanted me to believe that I was all alone. There were times when I felt like the Devil would not leave me alone. It became essential for me to remember that God is always with me. I learned that with God, I know that nothing could separate me from God's love, which is still present, no matter what I am going through.

My spiritual walk has allowed me the opportunity to seek wholeness. My wholeness will expose me to more attacks from the Devil. Therefore, the importance of keeping up my guard is highly relative. There is nothing more the Devil would love than destroying a believer. With my guard up, Christ empowered me to combat all the Devil's attacks.

THE IMPORTANCE OF HUMILITY

One of the highest human characteristics is humility. Nothing will take you lower than pride. Nothing will lift you higher than humility. Humility is one of the most critical attributes of growth. Being humble helps build trust and facilitates learning, which are vital aspects of spiritual and personal development.

Genuine gratitude and the lack of arrogance, an unpretentious view of oneself, characterize humility in many instances. Biblically, humility means a critical and continuous emphasis on godliness. We should be humble followers of Christ and trust in God's wisdom and salvation; we should also humble ourselves before our Creator for the gift of life given us.

An excellent summation of the meaning of humility comes from Proverbs 3:5–6 (NIV). These profound verses tell us,

> "Trust in the Lord with all your heart and lean not on your own understanding; in all your ways submit to him, and he will make your paths straight."

Furthermore, these verses tell us that we can demonstrate our humbleness by having faith in God to lead us in the best way to live and how to avoid temptation. It is essential for us to put complete trust in the Lord and that we do not deceive ourselves with vanity and lust. We must lean on God's understanding, wisdom, and divinity to direct us to the righteous path through faithful practices, such as prayer, meditation, fasting, and others. To open our hearts and withdraw from our ego's arrogance, we must have the initial requirement of humility.

Proverbs 22:4 (NIV) gives us a more in-depth look into the biblical meaning of humility through a concise description. "Humility is the fear of the Lord." Being humble is more than trusting God and following His will. It also includes dreading the outcomes of disregarding His commands for truth, love, work ethic, mercy, and beyond. Humility recognizes the high power of God and the potential vengeance He will reprimand us for if we do not direct our purpose toward righteousness.

APPLICATIONS

My philosophy as a lifelong learner is that theory (knowledge) plus application equals learning. This means that there is no evidence of learning if you cannot appropriately demonstrate/apply the theory (knowledge). With this said, I have gained so much knowledge through my search for spiritual growth. However, I needed to demonstrate my learning. Therefore, I designed an "Applications" section.

The purpose of this section is to assist others on their incredible journey. I compiled information that can be used to get you to monitor your spiritual growth. Please note that the included information merely suggestions. Know that you are the driver for your growth and what worked for me might not work for you.

Be blessed on your journey!

Starting point.

WHERE DO I START?

Our spiritual growth is highly impacted by our spiritual discernment. Verrett (2020) defined discernment as an eagerness to learn from those who are older and wiser. She denoted that true discernment starts with prayer. Reaching out to God in prayer, seeking guidance from wise believers, and studying the scripture helps develop a spirit of discernment. The ability to apply this wisdom is what makes a difference in the life of a believer. The more understanding and insight a Christian exerts, the stronger their faith and the better they will be able to ascertain what is good, right, and the will of God. As a result, the believer can demonstrate a love for God and others, just like Jesus did.

Spiritual discernment is an array of wisdom that comes from intuition as well as from learned experience and knowledge. Deriving from the Holy Spirit, spiritual discernment is a way of possessing understanding in deciding the genuine nature of a situation, person, or thing. Spiritual discernment focuses on Jesus and making decisions that align with those of Jesus within the New Testament. It is focusing on God and Jesus when making decisions that separate spiritual discernment from worldly discernment.

There are five steps of discernment: identifying the issue, taking time to pray about the choice, making a wholehearted decision, discussing the choice with a mentor, and then finally trusting the decision made.

The scripture provides evidence as to the reason for us to have spiritual discernment (1 John 5:19 NIV). Furthermore, the scriptures remind us of the fact that we must grow to be able to differentiate good from evil (Hebrews 5:11–14 NIV). Therefore, through practice, we can get better at discerning truth from error.

Our spiritual growth is predicated upon us knowing the truth. Studying God's Word (the Holy Bible) is the only way for us to gain the truth. On our journey to developing spirituality, we must be aware of the many false apostles and prophets disguising themselves as servants of righteousness. Scripture warns of these false apostles and prophets who are continually attempting to carry away those who are always studying but never able to apply the truth" (2 Timothy 3:7 NIV). It might be a challenge to match wits with these false apostles and prophets, but we can expose them by referring them to the obedience test found in the scripture (1 John 2:4).

We start with prayer and reading the Bible!

Start with prayer and reading the Bible.

FIVE STAGES OF SPIRITUAL GROWTH

The Bible teaches that there are five spiritual growth stages. We all are at one of these stages. There are many benefits to knowing the stages of spiritual growth. Being aware of these stages can help us grow personally and develop in our maturity. A brief description of each stage is below.

Stage 1: The Seeker

In this stage, the person is spiritually dead. Spiritually dead means that the person is a nonbeliever. Stage 1 incorporates the notion that we all start in life "dead in our transgressions and sins" (Ephesians 2:1). This notion signifies that we are separated from God and will experience an eternal death away from God unless we believe in Jesus Christ for salvation. As a spiritually dead person, we need a healthy relationship with a maturing believer. We need to be able to explain the message within the Gospel and an invitation to receive Christ. Nonbelievers are continually seeking answers to questions, such as "What is my purpose in life?" "What is going to happen to me after death?" and "Why are so many good people suffering if there is a God?"

Stage 2: The Believer

After a seeker is transformed and accepts Christ as their Savior, the person immediately enters Stage 2. As a believer, the person has entered spiritual infancy. The person understands that something has changed and is excited about sharing with others about it. The believers possess vast knowledge, but they lack the understanding of how to live as followers of Christ. Therefore, a new believer in Christ needs support from a mature believer. For example, the new believer will need explanations of the fundamental truths found in the Gospel and understand and model a growing believer's practices.

Step 3: The Learner

As the believer grows, they move into Stage 3, the spiritual child. This childlike spiritual stage appears throughout the Bible (1 John 2:12; 1 Corinthians 13:11). The Learner Stage is where a person is excited about their faith. Yet the person is still rebellious and self-centered in many ways. The learner tends to do what they should only when rewarded or threatened with some punishment. In many instances, the person may do the right thing. However, it is usually to avoid a disliked outcome or to get something they want. There are needs of the learner that must be met for them to continue to grow. These needs include instruction and modeling on how to feed themselves spiritually, recognize who they are in Christ, understand how to have fellowship with Christ and other believers, and grasp the notion of what are reasonable expectations relating to other believers.

Stage 4: The Server

The Learner grows and matures into the spiritual young adult stage. This stage is called the Server (1 John 2:13). At this stage, the believer has developed a decent grasp of God's Word. The server has become service oriented, God centered, and mission minded. However, the Server is not focusing on producing disciples. The Server has a great desire to serve, help, bless, and make their life count. The Server wants to make an impact and be of service to others. The server has some needs to move to the next stage. These needs include a place to learn to serve and a spiritual parent who will debrief them about the ministry experiences. These ongoing relationships offer encouragement and accountability, guidance on their expectations regarding how-to serve, who to serve, when to serve, etc., and assistance in recognizing and developing their spiritual gifts.

Stage 5: The Leader

The final stage of spiritual development is the Leader. We enter this stage when we become spiritually mature enough to reproduce disciples. As though we have become spiritual parents, we have become the Leaders (1 Corinthians 4:15, 17; 1 Thessalonians 2:11; 1 John 2:13–14). There is a significant difference between the Server and the Leader. As the spiritual parent, the leader focuses on how to help others grow through the stages to reach Stage 5. The server focuses on simply blessing others without any concern about assisting others to grow through the stages. As a Leader, you want to lead others to Christ and help new believers in their spiritual maturity. Furthermore, the Leader tends to be intentional and strategic about their role. Leaders have needs that include continuous relationships with other leaders, a church family, and encouragement.

SPIRITUAL GOALS: WHAT ARE THEY, AND WHY DO THEY MATTER?

Spiritual Goals: Definition and Importance

A goal is a desired outcome that you want to happen and work to reach. Spiritual goals are no different from any other plans. It is like setting a target up for yourself; it helps mark the direction you want to aim.

Why do I need spiritual goals?

So many of us drift when it comes to spirituality; we go with the flow. Some people will do as told to do—they go to church, read their scripture, they pray at prescribed times. Other people roam around aimlessly; they ask questions that only lead to more problems. They wonder about it all but reach no conclusions. Developing goals helps you grow and evolve; it keeps you from getting stuck in a spiritual rut.

What kinds of spiritual goals should I set?

Goals are our own business to determine. Asking myself where I want to be in a year or five or ten years is an excellent place to start. Another good idea for goals is to plan specific things you want to explore, nurture, or practice your spirituality. Spiritual goals are different for everyone. No one can tell you what your spiritual goals should be. However, based on my experience, I am offering some suggestions that might point in the direction.

A. Explore your own beliefs. Think of the biggest questions you want to be answered and determine you will spend the next few months researching, reflecting, and meditating on answers.

Keep a notebook or a journal as a record for this venture so that you can write down your evolving thoughts and feelings.

B. Plan to incorporate routines in your life. By routines, I mean small, repeated, daily acts that relate to your spirituality.

Establishing routines is a great way to get the mind to switch into that spiritual mode. Plan to keep up small but meaningful efforts, such as mealtime prayers, evening meditation, scripture reading, or chanting—whatever makes you feel spiritual.

C. Search for or join a group. A church can serve as a group, but it does not have to be. The group's focus should be spiritual, and it should be a religion or a practice with which you are comfortable. Having a group can be a great motivator and help keep you on track.

D. Start incorporating your religion's tenets more firmly in your life. Begin to practice what you preach. If you feel that overindulgence in unhealthy things or obsession with frivolous things like video games blocks your spiritual progress, begin letting go of your vices. It would be best to decide to start living the life you want to live and that you think is right to live.

Every now and then, you may want to reevaluate your spiritual goals to see how far you have come and how far you need to go. Change will not happen overnight, but start making small changes to work up to your goals.

KEYS FOR DEVELOPING SPIRITUAL DISCERNMENT

Developing spiritual discernment is hugely significant. In the world today, there are logical explanations for various religious beliefs. Some of these beliefs are opposed to each other. How do we acquire the spiritual discernment required to resolve how to worship God as He commands?

Treybig (2020) provides us with seven keys to help us develop spiritual discernment.

Key 1: Spiritual absolutes must be recognized.

Absolutes are fundamental in developing spiritual discernment as it is in almost every walk of life. Many people want to use their judgment to determine what is right and wrong, even with God's laws and morality. These people rebuff the fact that God is the authority over our lives. God offers explicit directions for us to follow, regardless of the situation. Identifying opposing and contrasting views is a form of discernment (i.e., clean versus unclean, good versus evil, right versus wrong, and obedience versus disobedience). Support for this thinking is in the scripture (Genesis 19:9; Matthew 7:1–3; John 7:24).

Key 2: Ask God for help.

Accepting that we do know everything we need to know is also fundamental for developing spiritual discernment. Today's popular shouts to simply follow your heart or look inside yourself to answer life's questions are not biblically correct. Scripture offers evidence of this key's importance (1 Kings 3:7, 9; Proverbs 14:12; 16:25; Jeremiah 10:23; 17:9).

Key 3: Imitate God. Hate what God hates; love what God loves.

God created man in His image. God desired for us to eventually become like Him (Romans 8:29; Philippians 3:21). Our values, thinking, and judgment will become more and more like God's as we grow in discernment. We might ask, "What should we imitate about God?" We must hate what God hates and love what God loves. This provides us a good starting place. Be reminded that God loves all people and wants everyone to be a member of His family. Scriptures highlight the things God loves (2 Corinthians 9:7; Revelation 5:8; Hebrews 13:16; Luke 12:32). However, He also hates sin because of the toll it takes upon humankind (John 3:15–17, 2 Peter 3:9, Romans 6:23). Scripture also highlights other things that God hates (Deuteronomy 12:31; 16:22; 22:5; Malachi 2:16; Leviticus 11:11; Proverbs 6:16–19; 11:1; 12:22; 15:9).

Key 4: Seek counsel.

Seeking advice from people who have wisdom and experience is another key that can help us make sound judgments. We must seek counsel from people who possess the knowledge, experience, and wisdom to give us the appropriate advice. Talking with our friends who may not have the expertise to provide adequate counsel will probably not provide knowledgeable answers and positive outcomes. King Solomon highlighted this key in several of his proverbs (Proverbs 11:14; 12:15; 15:22, Kings 4:34; 10:4)

Key 5: Practice making good judgments.

When we want to become better at a skill or hobby, we practice using the best techniques. In many instances, we devote a lot of time to practicing. Therefore, the more we practice, the better we become. We are all familiar with the cliche "Practice makes perfect." This cliche also applies if we want to develop spiritual discernment. More than reading about it is needed. We must do it. An illustration of this point can be found in the book of Hebrews (Hebrews 5:14).

Key 6: Choose your friends carefully.

The people highly influencing our thinking and actions are the ones we choose to include in our surroundings. You cannot choose your family, but you can most definitely choose your friends, so choose wisely. We discover that when we chose to surround ourselves with people who shared our spiritual values, we are encouraged to remain faithful to God. Fellowshipping with believers is so important. Fellowshipping with believers promotes growth in our love and respect for each other and God. Evidence of this key's importance is throughout the scriptures (Proverb 12:26; 1 Corinthians 15:33; Ephesians 5:11; 2 Corinthians 6:14; Hebrews 10:24; Acts 2:42; 1 John 1:3).

Key 7: Learn from your mistakes.

We all have made some mistakes and will continue to make mistakes. When we make mistakes, we sin! However, the most important thing is what we do after we sin. God wants us to repent for any ungodly acts that we commit and then return to following His commands. Scripture speaks to our tenacity in the face of mistakes (Proverbs 24:16; 1 Kings 8:46; 2 Chronicles 6:36; Ecclesiastes 7:20). We must always remember that "we fall down but we get up!" We need to learn from our mistakes, so we do not fall as often.

How to Create a
Spiritual Growth Plan

A Spiritual Growth Plan is a carefully thought and written plan that describes your belief about what God expects you to do to walk with Him and grow spiritually. Because of God, we grow, but it is our responsibility to put ourselves in a position to succeed. To nurture our spiritual life, God designed specific resources and discipline for us to use as "means of grace." A Spiritual Growth Plan is only thinking through and personalizing how we will incorporate these things into our lives. I would encourage you to consider the spiritual growth steps outlined below prayerfully. Allow God to speak to you about how He wants you to grow spiritually.

Five Steps to a Spiritual Growth Plan

1. Consider why spiritual growth is essential.

    Growing closer to God is an integral part of any Christian's life. Let these reasons why spiritual growth is so essential compel you to make spiritual growth a priority in your life. We must move beyond an absolute intro-level faith (Hebrew 5:11–14) and not just exist but to aim to win (1 Corinthians 9:24–27). We need to consistently move toward growth if we want God's most profound wisdom (Proverbs 2:1–11; Mark 4:24–25). Continual spiritual growth and connection with God are imperative. We need the two things to best use our spiritual gifts (John 15:1–8). We must keep in mind that our spiritual growth is not a one-time thing but an ongoing journey. God's endless love for us requires us to grow (2 Corinthians 5:14–15).

2. Pray, asking God to show you the areas you need to change or grow.

   Ask yourself, "What areas of my current life circumstances need change?"

   Here are some ideas to get you started. What are your answers to the following questions? Do you have specific faith or trust issues with God that you need to address? Do you feel a need to have more specific spiritual values, such as happiness, devotion, and calm, is evident in your life?

   Do you need specific character traits in your relationships, such as parenting, marriage, or friendships? Do you need to increase your knowledge and understanding of God or the Bible?

3. Determine what you need to grow spiritually.

4. Readily accept that spiritual growth and transformation often come at the most inconvenient times and in the most uncomfortable forms.

5. Acknowledge the fact that growth and transformation come a little at a time as we continue to seek God each day.

RECOGNIZING AND DEVELOPING SPIRITUAL GIFTS

When we become believers in Christ, the Holy Spirit fills us with gifts, such as wisdom, knowledge, faith, or even healing (1 Corinthians 12:8–11). We all have unique skills to work with, in conjunction with the body of Christ, so that we can bless and serve others.

An important question is "How do you acknowledge your gifts when you have difficulty identifying or using those gifts?" Perhaps you have accepted your skills but are not sure where or how to apply them.

Lazurek (2020) underscored eight ways to help you identify and develop your spiritual gifts.

1. Take an inventory.

    An excellent starting point is asking other believers what qualities they see in you. They have likely recognized God-given abilities that you have not recognized in yourself. Sometimes you might be unaware of your abilities simply because they have not been named. You can identify your gifts by spending time reflecting and in prayer. Seeking counsel from others is another way that can assist you in determining your talents. You can start by examining things that pique your interest.

2. Seek affirmation of your gifts from your community.

Ask the people within your faith community if they recognize your spiritual gifts. The people within your faith community will know you better than most other people. Therefore, they should be able to affirm your gifts. Declaring your blessings is a significant step for everyone in your group to take. If they cannot figure out your skills, take some time to pray as a group, and have the Holy Spirit help you identify your gifts.

3. Practice them.

If you do not use a skill, how will you know you have that gift? For those who know what your skills are, find your place within the church body and serve. Although you are sometimes needed to help in an area that is not your passion, it is possible to help and bring your love to your work.

If you are not serving currently, examine the available ministries that are within your church. Do any of these ministries jump out at you as areas of interest? Your heart may leap when you come across a ministry that resonates with what God has chosen to put on your heart.

4. Test them.

The church is the best place for putting your gifts to work. Engage your pastor in conversation about areas in which you can test your gifts. For example, you have identified hospitality as one of your gifts. However, you do not know what you are to do with this gift. Speak to your pastor about any upcoming events that could use that talent. It could be as simple as cooking food for a church potluck or assisting with the event's setup. It can also include making visitors feel welcome when they visit your church. It is essential to know that there is more to hospitality than greeting people or serving them food. The practice of making people feel welcome is integral to hospitality. If you can do this, you will quickly learn if this is the kind of service that energizes you.

5. Serve with them.

It is so easy to believe that church is a place for only being served a good sermon and then you go home. The Bible tells us that God's church is much more than that. Rather than being a buffet-style restaurant where you go, get filled, and then leave, the church is more of a potluck dinner where everyone brings something to the table that can bless another. When you are patient, God will reveal ways to connect and use your talents within the church.

Always collaborate your efforts with the ministry leader to ensure a need for the services you are willing to offer. Make sure that you are following the necessary policies and procedures that are in place. These procedures include respecting the leadership and working as you would work for the Lord. Remember what you do in service is truly a form of worship.

6. Analyze your gifts.

Give some serious thought to the talents that bring you the greatest joy. You can identify your gifts by evaluating the things that give you the most joy in many instances. The Holy Spirit has blessed us with the gifts of His choosing. We can depend on our natural learnings to understand how God wants us to use those gifts.

7. Praise God for your gifts.

We tend to take for granted all that God has blessed us with—including our gifts. We need to acknowledge our gifts and praise God for them. During your next prayer time, name your gifts. Be sure to thank God for each one. Do not shy away from gifts that others can identify that you never realized you possess. It is encouraging when others recognize your gifts.

8. Bless people with your gifts.

We need always to consider other ways to use our gifts to be blessings to others. For example, as an educator by profession, I teach others through my gift of overflow. I have the gift of the love of learning. Therefore, I like to bless people by sharing my love of learning. I use this gift to encourage others who thought earning a college degree was impossible. It was so rewarding to help others achieve something they always thought about but did not know how to make the thought become a reality.

Spiritual gifts are the gifts that we did nothing to earn. However, gifts are useless if not put into practice. By practicing these principles, you will find that you are not only a blessing to your church, friends, and family. You are also glorifying the Almighty God who gave you these gifts, and you find a benefit for yourself as well.

SPIRITUAL GROWTH ASSESSMENT PROCESS*

Our spiritual journey as followers of Christ began the moment we admitted our personal sin and placed our trust in Christ as Savior and Lord. From that point until death or the return of Christ, our life's call is to grow in Christlikeness. Jesus summarizes the disciple's call in Mark 8:34 (NIV). "Whoever wants to be my disciple must deny themselves and take up their cross and follow me." Accomplishing such a challenging assignment requires growing in your understanding of what it means to be a Christian, expanding your personal knowledge of biblical truth, and applying daily what you learn. Through the presence of His indwelling Spirit, God enables you to know, obey, and serve Him. God expects His children to grow spiritually, and His Word encourages personal examination as an element of growth.

Ephesians 4:12–15 (NIV) highlights a call for us to attain a mature fullness. This call carries a promise of stability and joy for our Christian experience. However, this promise is only fulfilled as we respond with a sincere desire and to grow spiritually. A personal spiritual inventory has been adapted to help you assess areas of spiritual growth that you might want to address. Clearly, a simple test cannot measure how "spiritual" we are; however, this assessment can serve as a tool to suggest next steps in your journey toward spiritual maturity.

Getting Started

Rate each of the following statements to the best of your ability. If you are unsure of the appropriate response, follow your first impulse. It is usually your best attempt. Remember there are no right or wrong responses. These statements are provided as indicators as to where you might want to grow spiritually. Read each statement and enter a number in the "Response" column indicating how much you agree with the statement listed as it pertains to your spiritual life.

This assessment process can help you complete an examination and careful search of your spiritual growth. Follow these simple steps to complete the process:

1. Complete the Spiritual Growth Assessment. The assessment helps you think carefully about your spiritual development related to six specific spiritual disciplines: abiding in Christ, living in the Word, praying in faith, fellowshipping with believers, witnessing to the world, and ministering to others. Before completing your responses, ask the Lord to guide your evaluation. Since most of these statements require a subjective response, His guidance is the key to an accurate appraisal. Also, resist the urge to compare scores with others. Self-condemnation or pride could result from such comparisons. Trust God to help you grow spiritually by revealing heart issues and empowering you to act.

2. Chart your responses on the chart provided. Use the chart to identify the areas where you may need to focus. Use this information to develop an action plan.

3. Begin working on a personal growth plan. The spiritual growth plan worksheet helps you formulate an intentional plan for growth. As you discuss your plan with a mature believer, you may discover additional actions that more effectively meet your needs. Remember becoming like Christ centers

on His work in us and not our work for Him. God desires heart changes over religious actions. Without question, God does the revealing, the renewing, the empowering, and the recreating. Your part as His disciple is to do the yielding, the submitting, and the obeying. Please note that your plan will continually change as you grow.

Second Corinthians 13:5 says, "Examine yourselves as to whether you are in the faith. Test yourselves. Do you not know yourselves, that Jesus Christ is in you?—unless indeed you are disqualified." We are saved by grace, through faith, not by works, lest any man should boast. When we have Christ in us, at work producing His righteousness in us, this has a real effect. Just as the presence of a virus in our bodies can be detected by our physical symptoms, so can our spiritual well-being. Do you have a committed relationship with Jesus? Are you spiritually mature? Come find out!

As you complete the assessment, avoid rushing. Listen for God's voice to encourage and challenge you. Consider this experience as one-on-one time with Him. Be intentional in your growth toward Christlikeness.

SPIRITUAL GROWTH INVENTORY

Use the scale below to respond to each statement.

Never 1	Seldom 2	Occasionally 3	Frequent 4	Always 5
Spiritual Disciplines				Response
Abide in Christ.				
1. I practice a regular quiet time and look forward to that time with Christ.				
2. When making choices, I seek Christ's guidance first.				
3. My relationship with Christ is motivated more by love than duty or fear.				
4. I experience life change because of my worship experiences.				
5. When God makes me aware of His specific will in an area of my life, I follow His leading.				
6. I believe Christ provides the only way for a relationship with God.				
7. My actions demonstrate a desire to build God's kingdom rather than my own.				
8. Peace, contentment, and joy characterize my life rather than worry and anxiety.				
9. I trust Christ to help me through any problem or crisis I face.				
10. I remain confident of God's love and provision during difficult times.				
Total				

Live in the Word.	
1.	I regularly read and study my Bible.	
2.	I believe the Bible is God's Word and provides His instructions for life.	
3.	I evaluate cultural ideas and lifestyles by biblical standards.	
4.	I can answer questions about life and faith from a biblical perspective.	
5.	I replace impure or inappropriate thoughts with God's truth.	
6.	I demonstrate honesty in my actions and conversation.	
7.	Generally, my public and private self are the same.	
8.	I use the Bible as the guide for the way I think and act.	
9.	I study the Bible for the purpose of discovering truth for daily living.	
Total	

Pray in faith.	
1.	My prayers focus on discovering God's will more than expressing my needs.	
2.	I trust God to answer when I pray and wait patiently on His timing.	
3.	My prayers include thanksgiving, praise, confession, and requests.	
4.	I expect to grow in my prayer life and intentionally seek help to improve.	
5.	I spend as much time listening to God as talking to Him.	
6.	I pray because I am aware of my complete dependence on God for everything in my life.	
7.	Regular participation in group prayer characterizes my prayer life.	
8.	I maintain an attitude of prayer throughout each day.	
9.	I believe my prayers impact my life and the lives of others.	
10.	I engage in a daily prayer time.	
Total	

Fellowship with believers.	
1. I forgive others when their actions harm me.	
2. I admit my errors in relationships and humbly seek forgiveness from the one I've hurt.	
3. I allow other Christians to hold me accountable for spiritual growth.	
4. I seek to live in harmony with other members of my family.	
5. I place the interest of others above my self-interest.	
6. I am gentle and kind in my interactions with others.	
7. I encourage and listen to feedback from others to help me discover areas for relationship growth.	
8. I show patience in my relationships with family and friends.	
9. I encourage others by pointing out their strengths rather than criticizing their weaknesses.	
10. My time commitments demonstrate that I value relationships over work/career/hobbies.	
Total	

Witness to the world.	
1. I share my faith in Christ with nonbelievers.	
2. I regularly pray for nonbelievers I know.	
3. I make my faith known to my neighbors and/or fellow employees.	
4. I intentionally maintain relationships with nonbelievers to share my testimony.	
5. When confronted about my faith, I remain consistent and firm in my testimony.	
6. I help others understand how to effectively share a personal testimony.	
7. I make sure the people I witness to get the follow-up and support needed to grow in Christ.	
8. I encourage my church and friends to support mission efforts.	
9. I am prepared to share my testimony at any time.	
10. My actions demonstrate a belief in and commitment to the Great Commission (Matthew 28:19–20).	
Total	

Minister to others.	
1. I understand my spiritual gifts and use those gifts to serve others.	
2. I serve others, expecting nothing in return.	
3. I sacrificially contribute my finances to help others in my church and community.	
4. I go out of my way to show love to people I meet.	
5. Meeting the needs of others provides a sense of purpose in my life.	
6. I share biblical truth with those I serve as God gives opportunity.	
7. I act as if others' needs are as important as my own.	
8. I expect God to use me every day in His kingdom work.	
9. I regularly contribute time to a ministry at my church.	
10. I help others identify ministry gifts and become involved in ministry.	
Total	

*Adapted from https://www.lifeway.com/en/articles/women-leadership-spiritual-gifts-growth-service.

SPIRITUAL GROWTH ASSESSMENT CHART

Please enter the totals for each of the areas from the Spiritual Growth Assessment. Use the totals to answer the questions that follow to design an action plan.

Discipline	Response Total
Abiding in Christ	
Living in the Word	
Praying in Faith	
Fellowshipping with Believers	
Witnessing to the World	
Ministering to Others	

In the space provided, answer the following questions:

1. Which of the six disciplines of spiritual development appears to be your strongest?

   _____

2. List one benefit this strength serves for

   a. you personally: _____

   b. your family: _____

   c. your church: _____

   d. your community: _____

3. Which of the six disciplines of spiritual development appears to require the most attention?

   _____

4. List one reward that growth in these disciplines would bring to

   a. you personally: _____

   b. your family: _____

   c. your church: _____

   d. your community: _____

5. What action steps do you need to take to improve in spiritual development that requires the most attention?

   _____

6. Share your goal with someone who will keep you on track with your objectives.

7. Who will be your encouragement partner in this process?

   _____

Score Interpretation

- A score of 51–60 means you are well-developed in this area. Keep up the good work!
- A score of 41–50 means you are doing well in this area, but there is still opportunity for deeper growth. Look back to see if there were questions that had low scores to get some insight into specific areas you might want to give attention to.
- A score of 31–40 means that you are on your way and still have some opportunity for significant growth in this area.
- A score of 21–30 means the foundation is being firmed up and you still have some opportunity for significant growth in this area.
- A score of 11–20 means a foundation is being built and you still have some opportunity for significant growth in this area.
- A score of 10 or below indicates that this is an area that would be a great place to seek growth in this year.

NEXT STEP: TAKE ACTION

You are now ready to develop a plan for how you will pursue growth in a specific area in a specific area in the next year. Seek out a study group, commit to read books on the topic, or ask a mature believer to partner with you in praying for growth.

A template is supplied for use in devising your spiritual growth plan.

MY SPIRITUAL GROWTH PLAN

I started my Spiritual Growth Plan on _____.

Step 1: Create my Spiritual Growth Plan.

Using the data from the assessment form, establish a specific goal in the area(s) you scored the lowest.

For the next three months, I will

1. improve my understanding of God's will for the following area of focus through individual or group study:

   _____.

2. My goal is _____.

For the next three months, I will

1. improve my understanding of God's will for the following area of focus through individual or group study:

   _____.

2. My goal is _____.

For the next three months, I will

1. improve my understanding of God's will for the following area of focus through individual or group study:

_____.

2. My goal is _____.

Step 2: Enlist a mature believer who will agree to

- meet with me to review my plan and pray with me about sticking with it
- meet with me at least once a month to discuss my progress
- celebrate my successes with me and challenge me to stay focused on my plan
- pray for me

I choose _____ as my mature believer.

REFERENCES

Daffern, J. (2020). "7 Keys to Knowing God's Will for Your Life: Make sure you what God is calling you to do." Retrieved from https://www.beliefnet.com/faiths/christianity/7-keys-to-knowing-gods-will-for-your-life.aspx.

Edwards, T. (2019). "What Does Spiritual Growth Actually Look Like?" Retrieved from https://www.relevantmagazine.com/faith/what-does-spiritual-growth-actually-look/.

Hertzenberg, S. (2020). "Why It's Okay to Have Questions about Your Faith." Retrieved from https://www.beliefnet.com/faiths/why-its-okay-to-have-questions-about-your-faith.aspx.

Lazurek, M. (2020). "8 Ways to Recognize and Develop Your Spiritual Gifts." Retrieved from https://www.ibelieve.com/faith/ways-to-recognize-and-develop-your-spiritual-gifts.html.

Spiritual Growth Assessment Process. Retrieved from https://www.lifeway.com/en/articles/women-leadership-spiritual-gifts-growth-service.

Treybig, D. (2020). "7 Keys for Developing Spiritual Discernment." Retrieved from https://lifehopeandtruth.com/life/christian-living/developing-spiritual-discernment/.

Verrett, B. (2020). "Understanding the Spiritual Gift of Discernment." Retrieved from https://www.biblestudytools.com/bible-study/topical-studies/understanding-the-spiritual-gift-of-discernment.html.

ANNOTATED BIBLIOGRAPHY

This annotated bibliography includes a list of books that helped me as I sought to grow spiritually.

Albom, M. (2003). *The Five People You Meet in Heaven*. New York, NY: Hyperion.
This book provides us an astounding story that will change your thoughts about the afterlife as well as the meaning of our lives here on earth.

Allen, J. (2020). *Get Out of Your Head: Stopping the Spiral of Toxic Thoughts*. Colorado Springs, CO: Westbrook.
The author encourages and prepares us to transform our lives by taking control of our thoughts. Our Enemy's goal is to get into our heads and make us feel ill-equipped to make advancements within the kingdom of God. However, when we submit our minds to Christ, the promises and goodness of God flood our lives in remarkable ways.

Coelho, P. (2014). *The Alchemist, 25th Anniversary: A Fable about Following Your Dream*. New York, NY: HarperCollins.
The author tells the mystical story of an Andalusian shepherd boy who desires to search for a worldly treasure. His travels teach us about the value of listening to our hearts, identifying the opportunity, learning to read the signs scattered along life's path, and most importantly, following our dreams.

Comer, J. M. (2019). *The Ruthless Elimination of Hurry: How to Stay Emotionally Healthy and Spiritually Alive in the Chaos of the Modern World*. Colorado Springs, CO: Waterbrook.
Comer provides us with a persuasive case for the value of a more straightforward way of life.

Cymbala, J. (2017). *Strong through the Storm: How to Be a Christian in the World Today*. Grand Rapids, MI: Zondervan.
Cymbala uses powerful stories of people who have been transformed by Christ to offer hope and help Christians to ascertain that a life submitted to Christ is not easily defeated, especially amid the growing hostility toward Christians. He highlights that nothing can suppress the Gospel's light, regardless of how much spiritual darkness encompasses the world.

Floyd, R. W. (2010). *The Power of Prayer and Fasting*. Nashville, TN: B&H Publishing.
The author explains prayer and fasting as a scripture-ordained act of obedience. The act is a way of humbling ourselves before God, growing closer to Him, and allowing God to speak and act in our lives. The book provides fascinating stories of the difference prayer and fasting have made in his and others' lives. The author highlighted compelling summations on how prayer and fasting work in a Christian's life. It also offers practical guidance for those who have never fasted before and a stirring call to revival.

Foster, R. J. (2018). *Celebration of Discipline, Special Anniversary Edition: The Path to Spiritual Growth*. New York, NY: HarperCollins.
This book explores the central spiritual practices called "Disciplines of the Christian Faith." Throughout this book, Foster heralds that the actual path to spiritual growth can be found only by and through these practices. He offers a plethora of examples substantiating how these disciplines can become part of our daily activities. These examples also demonstrate how the disciplines can help us shed our aimless practices and bring God's abundance into our lives.

Foster, R. J. (2010). *Life with God: Reading the Bible for Spiritual Transformation*. New York, NY: HarperCollins.

This book is an essential guide to approaching the Bible through the lens of Christian spiritual formation. It includes an abundance of examples and crucial yet straightforward insights revealing that reading the Bible for inward transformation is much different from reading the Bible for historical knowledge, literary appreciation, or religious instruction.

Foster, R. J. (2002). *Prayer: Finding the Heart's True Home*. New York, NY: HarperCollins.

Foster presents a powerful introduction to prayer. Through this convincing work, Foster helps us to understand the many forms of prayer. His work sheds light on the prayer process by addressing common misconceptions.

Foster, R. J. (2001). *Streams of Living Water: Celebrating the Great Traditions of Christian Faith*. New York, NY: HarperCollins.

In this work, Foster explores the six elements of faith and practice that define Christian tradition. He shows how a variety of ways are all essential elements of growth and maturity. Furthermore, Foster examines each tradition's distinctive aspects and offers compelling stories regarding faithful people whose lives categorized each element.

Franklin, J. (2020). *Acres of Diamonds: Discovering God's Best Right Where You Are*. Grand Rapids, MI: Chosen Books.

Have you ever experienced a place in your life where you felt you should be thriving only to be amazed by the sense of unfulfillment and you wanted to give up? Franklin provides us with a way to discover the endless God-given riches that lie around us. This book assists you in learning how to identify and cherish the potential hidden right where you are!

Jeremiah, D. (2019). *Everything You Need, Signature Edition with Devotions*. Nashville, TN: Thomas Nelson.

Drawing from biblical scriptures, the author explores eight critical tools the Lord provides—diligence, virtue, knowledge, self-control, perseverance, godliness, kindness, and love—to help you live boldly and confidently. The book also features an exclusive seven-day devotional.

Lucado, M. (2019). *How Happiness Happens: Finding Lasting Joy in a World of Comparison, Disappointment, and Unmet Expectations.* Nashville, TN: Thomas Nelson.
Living in a world where searching for happiness is a norm, the author offers a personalized plan for living a life filled with lasting and fulfilling joy, validated by Jesus's teaching and modern research.

Moore, Beth. (2020*). Chasing Vines: Finding Your Way to an Immensely Fruitful Life, Exclusive Edition.* Carol Stream, IL: Tyndale Momentum.
How does the field of your life feel? Is it like rocky soil? The author examines what it means to abide in the vine of Christ and bear abundant fruit. This book contains many personalized extras. This special edition includes insightful discussion questions. It also provides life application takeaways to allow you to dig deeper into God's plan for human flourishing. Also, for group or individual reflection, a study guide is included.

Moreland, J. P. (2012). *Love Your God with All Your Mind: The Role of Reason in the Life of the Soul.* Colorado Springs, CO: NavPress.
This book explains the importance of using your mind to win others to Christ and experience personal spiritual growth. The author challenges you to use logic and reason to further God's kingdom through evangelism, apologetics, worship, and vocation.

Nouwen, H. J., Christensen, M. J., and Laird, R. J. (2010). *Spiritual Formation: Following the Movements of the Spirit.* New York, NY: HarperCollins Publishers.
This book showcases the authors' effort to reconstruct the five classical stages of spiritual development as movements in the journey of faith. The book provides the readers with a spiritual formation

experience through the included readings, stories, personal reflection questions, and guided journal inquiry.

Schelske, M. A. (2017). *The Wisdom of Your Heart: Discovering the God-Given Purpose and Power of Your Emotions.* Colorado Springs, CO: David C. Cook.
Christians have various beliefs about emotions. Some Christians believe many myths about emotions. Emotions lead you astray. Emotions are not spiritual. God is not emotional—the biggest myth. Therefore, emotions are a God-given source of wisdom when we know how to interpret them. This book will provide a path for listening to the spiritual insights that your emotions offer every day.

Stanford, D. (2018). *Losing the Cape: The Power of Ordinary in a World of Superheroes.* Chicago, IL: Moody Publishers.
The author demonstrates that availability is more important than ability through inspiring stories from the Bible and his life with God. This book is an invitation to start making the world a better place through your ordinary, everyday presence.

Stanley, C. F. (2017). *The Gift of Heaven.* Nashville, TN: Nelson Books.
Dr. Stanley offers biblically based teaching and insights for anyone who has questions about God and what happens after we die.

Tolle, E. (2004). *The Power of Now: A Guide to Spiritual Enlightenment.* Vancouver, BC, Canada: Namaste Publishing, Inc.
This author allows the reader to embark upon an inspiring spiritual journey. This spiritual journey leads the readers to find their true and deepest self. By discovering truth and light, the reader will reach the ultimate in personal growth and spirituality.

Walters, K. N. (2019). *Soul Deep: A Biblical and Practical Guide to Healing Soul Wounds.* New York, NY: Soar Publishing House.
This book takes you through a process of transparency and self-evaluation to help you move beyond the disappointments, trauma, or

heartbreak you may have experienced. Using solid biblical principles with practical solutions, the author challenges you to remove the Band-Aids covering your wounded soul and receive the healing that will propel you into a glorious transformation.

Warren, R. (2104). *God's Answers to Life's Difficult Questions (Living with Purpose)*. Grand Rapids, MI: Zondervan.
By examining the lives of biblical characters, such as Moses, Paul, and Jesus, the author demonstrates how they dealt with circumstances with wisdom and faith in God. The book includes detailed, easy-to-comprehend insights that will assist you in moving past your obstacles and enjoying a purposeful, peaceful, and meaningful life.

Warren, R. (2014). *God's Power to Change Your Life (Living with Purpose)*. Grand Rapids, MI: Zondervan.
Warren draws simple but powerful truths from the Bible to provide practical guidance for specific types of change. It also links you up with the power to make the changes you long to make. Your life will change as you apply the truth of God's Word by the power of his Spirit.

Warren, R. (2013). *The Purpose Driven Life: What on Earth Am I Here For?* Grand Rapids, MI: Zondervan.
This book helps you understand the purpose of your life. The book can serve as the road map for your spiritual journey—a journey that will transform your life. It includes links to three-minute video introductions to each chapter and a thirty- to forty-minute audio Bible study message for each chapter. The book also contains appendixes, including questions for further study and additional resources.

Whitney, D. S. (2019). *How Can I Be Sure I'm a Christian? The Satisfying Certainty of Eternal Life*. Colorado Springs, CO: NavPress.
The author guides us through the Bible's teachings on salvation and eternal life. It steers us away from misplaced confidence and points us always toward Christ, who is our hope.

Whitney, D. S. (2014). *Spiritual Disciplines for the Christian Life.* Colorado Springs, CO: NavPress.
Whitney illustrates why the disciplines are essential. He shows how each one will help you grow in godliness. This book will provide you with a refreshing opportunity to become more like Christ and grow in character and maturity.

Whitney, D. S. (2014). *Spiritual Disciplines for the Christian Life Study Guide.* Colorado Springs, CO: NavPress.
This book is an updated companion guide to *Spiritual Disciplines for the Christian Life.* It guides you through a carefully selected array of disciplines that will help you grow in godliness. It is ideal for personal or small-group use.

Whitney, D. S. (2001). *Ten Questions to Diagnose Your Spiritual Health.* Colorado Springs, CO: NavPress.
This book emphasizes ten challenging questions that will lead you to look outside your spiritual activity to evaluate your spiritual health's actual state and help you on your spiritual transformation journey.

Acknowledgments

I would like to acknowledge the following:

- my parents, the late William Fisher Thomas Sr. and the late Thelma Henderson Thomas, for their unconditional love and teachings
- my son, Lamond, for always pushing me toward spirituality in his own special way
- my five siblings for their encouragement and support throughout all my endeavors
- my granddaughter, Amyah, for being my change agent; thank you for your persistence and many invitations to come to church with you
- the 150 people (most of them relatives) who lived in Beulah, Mississippi, who prescribed to the notion that "It takes a village to raise a child"
- Dr. Willie Powell for being such an inspiration. Your eagerness for learning and willingness to share your wisdom will be forever treasured
- the Proviso Missionary Baptist Church Family for your welcoming spirit and your inclination to accept all who come
- Bishop Dr. Claude Porter and Pastor John F. Harrell for providing me with opportunities to serve others
- all my friends and extended family members for traveling on my journey with me; you all will never really know just how much I treasure our relationships.

About the Author

D. Dianna Thomas, Ph.D., a native of Beulah, Mississippi, describes herself as a lifelong learner. She graduated from West Bolivar District one High School in Rosedale, Mississippi. She received a Bachelor of Arts in Applied Behavioral Science (Management) from National-Louis University of Evanston, Illinois. D. Dianna earned a Master of Education specializing in Special Education from National-Louis University of Evanston, Illinois. She completed a Master of Arts degree from Concordia University of Chicago, Illinois, specializing in Educational Leadership. D. Dianna also earned a Doctor of Philosophy (Ph.D.) degree from Capella University of Minneapolis, Minnesota, specializing in Special Education Leadership.

D. Dianna has worked in the field of education as paraprofessional, special education teacher, and administrator for over four decades. D. Dianna is an avid reader, enjoys studying the Word of God, spectator sports, and being a grandmother.